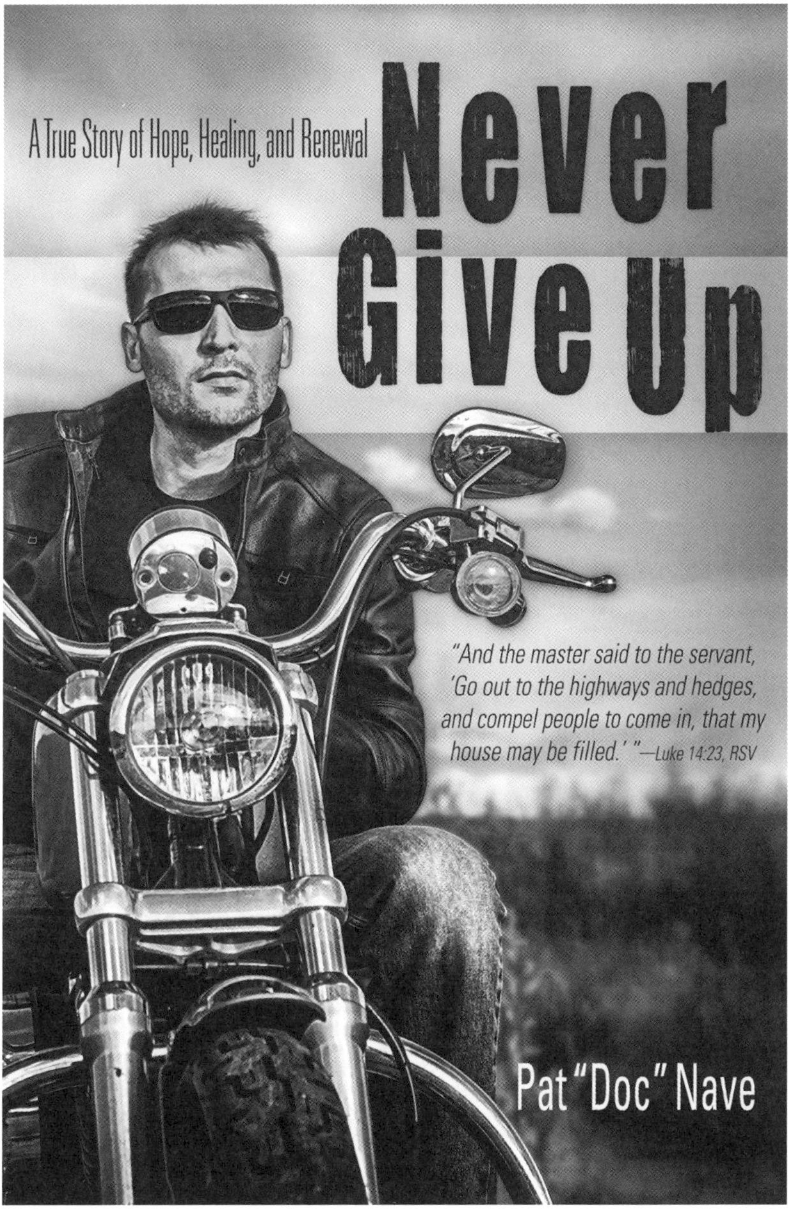

Never Give Up

A True Story of Hope, Healing, and Renewal

"And the master said to the servant, 'Go out to the highways and hedges, and compel people to come in, that my house may be filled.'" —Luke 14:23, RSV

Pat "Doc" Nave

Pacific Press®
Publishing Association

Nampa, Idaho | Oshawa, Ontario, Canada
www.pacificpress.com

Cover design by Steve Lanto
Cover design resources from istockphoto.com
Inside design by Kristin Hansen-Mellish

Copyright © 2015 by Pacific Press® Publishing Association
Printed in the United States of America
All rights reserved.

The author assumes full responsibility for the accuracy of all facts and quotations as cited in this book.

Unless otherwise noted, Scripture quotations are taken from the New King James Version®. Copyright © 1982 by Thomas Nelson, Inc. Used by permission. All rights reserved.

Scriptures quoted from RSV are from the Revised Standard Version of the Bible, copyright © 1946, 1952, 1971 by the Division of Christian Education of the National Council of the Churches of Christ in the U.S.A. Used by permission.

You can obtain additional copies of this book by calling toll-free 1-800-765-6955 or by visiting http://www.adventistbookcenter.com.

Library of Congress Cataloging-in-Publication Data:

Nave, Pat, 1965-
 Never give up : a true story of hope, healing, and renewal / Pat "Doc" Nave.
    pages cm
 ISBN 13: 978-0-8163-5713-0 (pbk.)
 ISBN 10: 0-8163-5713-7 (pbk.)
1. Nave, Pat, 1965- 2. Seventh-day Adventist converts—United States—Biography. 3. Drug traffic—United States. I. Title.
BX6189.N38A3 2015
286.7092—dc23
[B]
                              2014044727

January 2015

Contents

Preface	5
1: The Heritage of the Yuck	9
2: Dad's Early Years	13
3: Mom and Dad Try to Move Forward	17
4: Prison	21
5: Tug-of-War	24
6: The Great Escape	26
7: Moving to Florida	30
8: The Potential Drug Dealer	35
9: Extradited	40
10: The Heritage	44
11: Drifting In and Out	48
12: Running From God	55
13: Fear	62
14: Pleasing God . . . Earning Love?	67
15: Japan	72
16: No Trust in Anyone	75
17: Satan Is Real . . . But God Is All-Powerful	79
18: The Seeds of a Motorcycle Outreach	86
Epilogue: Where I Am Today	90

Preface

"Will you accept the charges?"

I stood there with the telephone in hand. Hearing my father's voice in the background, I informed the operator that I would accept the charges and waited for the *click,* signifying she was off the line. Now free to speak without the filter of Bell Telephone, what my father told me would change my life forever. "Son, you have to protect our home."

I knew what that meant because for the last couple of years my father had taught me what I was to do if things got out of hand. I was to go into his bedroom, look under the bed, and take out the guns he had placed there. I was to load them up, walk calmly into the living room, turn over the couch, squat behind it, and watch the front door. "If the doorknob moves, just start firing." He concluded his directions with, "When you are finished, take the guns, wipe off your fingerprints, go out the back door to the canal, drop the guns into the canal, and run—run as fast and as far away as you can. Then call Paul in North Carolina, and he will come get you."

As I stood there with the receiver pressed to my ear, it was clear that the time had come. I must protect my mother and brothers. I know it seems strange hearing a tale like this, but my life was far from normal.

My father had risen in the ranks of the South Florida mob, and as a result, I had been introduced to people of various abilities and talents. There was Mike, the jeweler who ran a mob-funded diamond company. Mike had served time in place of a high-ranking mob official, and in return was given a successful company upon his release from prison. Bud, who became my godfather, ran the mob operations up to the Tennessee border, lived in a townhome, and ran pig farms to launder his money. Stubs had gotten caught cheating the mob and had his pinky cut off as a reminder of what would happen to him if he ever chose that route again.

Then there was Alfredo, the crazed Cuban who lived to party. It was Alfredo who hired me at the ripe old age of fourteen to work at one of his furniture stores and later at an auto body shop in Miami. I delivered furniture with Rafael, an explosives and weapons expert.

On weekends when Alfredo was bored, he would rent part of a hotel on Miami Beach and we would all party and eat until we simply could not move. Alfredo was insane. He would light firecrackers and bottle rockets inside his house, and you would have to stay on your toes to avoid the line of fire. He always had a Michelob beer in his hand, and you could tell from the tint of his eyes that alcohol was probably not the only substance coursing through his body.

Adding to the palette of colorful people in my life was the limping insurance guy who tried to have me killed, the politician who convinced my dad that he should fly down to Colombia and pick up yet another shipment of drugs, and the crooked sheriff's deputy who partied with my dad when it was convenient—and at times when it was not. These were all people without morals, people intent on making money in an industry that was highly illegal.

My father's mob name was "Peter Rabbit." I'm not sure how he got it, but it stuck, and it made him somewhat of a fairy tale to me. I was intrigued by his power, afraid of his temper, and was introduced to a world that many only faintly know about through books and television. My father once told me that the only way someone could even begin to understand what his life was like was to watch the movie *Scarface* with Al Pacino.

I knew all too well what life in the mob was all about. We lived in a shroud of secrecy, drove stolen cars, kept the blinds shut because my father didn't trust anyone, and never had a friend come into our home. We were raised in darkness. Discipline involved my dad beating us with a horse whip when we were smaller and throwing a knife at us when we got older. He would always miss, of course, but it sent the fear of death crackling like lightning into our souls. We knew better than to disobey, and seeds were planted deep within us that if we stepped out of line, we would be severely punished.

On one particular occasion, my father wanted to drive his point deep within me, so with a 9mm Beretta pistol in his hand, he proceeded to shoot off the clip around the house with me sitting right beside him. To this day, I am not sure how it was that he missed me. When he was done, he simply said, "So, I suppose you will call the police now." Of course that was the furthest thing from my mind because I knew that if I ever turned my father in, there would be no escaping his reach, even from the inside of a prison cell. I loved him greatly but feared him more than any person alive.

The night he asked me to defend our home, he had been arrested by the FBI. Agent Donahue had left his business card on our dining room table, and my dad had informed me that some other people were going to try to harm our family. I followed his request and set the plan in motion. I moved the cars out into the darkness, grabbed my dad's sawed-off shotgun and a few other guns, flipped the couch over, and for hours stared at the front door. If that doorknob had budged even slightly, I would have filled the door with holes.

But it didn't. Instead, I stayed up all night afraid that I would have to shoot; afraid that I would have to kill. Part of me was cocky with excitement about the possibilities, adrenaline flowing; and a part of me was deathly afraid. I am not sure of what my mother and grandmother made of the situation, but I was sure of one thing during those terrible years—I would never, ever let my father down.

As you can imagine, being raised in the home of a drug dealer skewed my fragile, developing mind. My attempts to live a "normal" life were complicated by my father throwing religion into the mix as his trump card. The result was a mixture of God and drugs that took my life from insane to psychedelic.

The book you are holding in your hands is my story. It is a story of addiction chasing me toward the very belly of hell. And it is a story of God reaching down and rescuing me—often against my will. I wish it were a figment of my imagination. But it all happened. However, the end result is that it has given me a deep and rich experience with the word *grace*. And for that, I am forever grateful to my Lord and Savior Jesus Christ.

I am writing this book, not because I am proud of my past, but because I believe that no matter our pasts, God can redeem us for His glory. There is always hope!

1: The Heritage of the Yuck

Every story has a beginning, and mine began less than spectacularly at St. Joseph's Hospital in Pontiac, Michigan, on June 6, 1965. My mother would gleefully cackle that I was supposed to be twin girls and that somehow I thwarted the doctors and came out as one boy. I would respond that I was apparently twice as good as any girl, but she never seemed convinced.

I entered the world as an innocent child, but if I could have vetoed the choice of my parents, I probably would have. I mean, who would want to be born into a drug dealer's family? The silver screen may make it sound cool, but there was not much silver in the screen of my life. My father was born to Nina and Mack Nave from Protem, Missouri. Protem is a little hamlet in southern Missouri near the border of Arkansas.

My grandfather Mack was a gruff and demanding man who had many brushes with the law, and who didn't think twice about cheating on his wife. When he was arrested and on his way to prison, he escaped and spent the rest of his life dodging the law. Soon he was also dodging cancer. Both finally caught up with him.

I had no idea about my grandfather's life until I picked up a Leeper, Michigan, newspaper one day. The front page announced that it was the anniversary of the arrest of the dangerous outlaw Mack Nave. He had died before I was born, and from the stories of his craziness, I figured that he was a rebel. Apparently, he was a rebel and a fugitive.

A favorite story about my grandfather as a young man centered around his father offering him a large sum of money and a ranch in Missouri. Mack, being the carefree type, turned him down and began to live as a drifter, in and out of trouble, always looking for the next great adventure.

It seemed Mack was born in the wrong century. He should have lived during the Civil War, when outlaws were rampant and the urge to head west filled many a young man with suspense. This urge for action, the unknown, and adventure lives in the DNA of the Nave clan. Never satisfied with the status quo, they are always seeking for that next adrenaline hit.

Growing up, my father had only one source of stability, his mom and my granny, Nina Maude Nave, quite possibly the toughest woman you could ever know. Somewhat like the tough-as-nails Granny Clampett on the TV show *The Beverly Hillbillies,* Granny Nina was tougher still, a bit heavier, and a bit more coarse. She carried a .38 pistol in her purse and had been known to brandish it when needed.

The memories of my granny were quite colorful. She was our doctor, sage, and do-it-all person. When I needed a tooth pulled, she would call over my uncle Joe and he would hold me down while she straddled me and took out her doctorin' tools—which in the case of tooth pullin' was a set of vise grips. She would latch on to the tooth and heave with all her might. The poor tooth never stood a chance. I learned early on never to complain about a loose tooth.

But she was more than a "dentist." In fourth grade, I made the mistake of growing a seed wart on the bottom of my foot. Looking for some pity, I complained, and before I knew it, my uncle had me pinned on the hood of her car. Granny had gotten out a knife and started doctorin' me right there on the spot. She dug into the wart, determined to eradicate it forever. There was no pain reliever, and if

I complained, my uncle was quick to question my manhood. I kept telling him that even a man would at least get a bullet to bite down on. He was not impressed and just told me to suck it up.

I grew up thinking that Granny had been a nurse. It wasn't until I was grown and married that I learned she got her doctorin' skills from working as a custodian at a mental hospital. If I had known that at the time, I would have been terrified of her, but in my ignorance, I was always in awe of her surgical magic.

One time, my older brother split open his foot on a bottle in the lake and Granny was called to fix it up. I imagined that he was going to be taken to the hospital, as there was blood everywhere, but not so. Granny got out her turpentine and rubbing alcohol; and before we knew it, she had a rag tied around Jim's foot and the healing had begun.

A few weeks later, she had to try her healing methods on my torn-up kneecap. At five years old, I had decided that I was Superman. Carefully placing a towel around my neck and securing it with a clothes pin, I dashed down the hillside behind our house before launching myself into the air. My certainty that I could fly came crashing down, along with my kneecap on a stump with an old rusty nail sticking out of it.

In agony, I once again made the mistake of howling, and Granny was quick to the rescue. She cleaned out the wound and for the rest of that summer I was placed on a lounge chair for my knee to heal. Strangely, it did actually heal. Of course, today I have this nice little scar to show for it, but in my mind, the legend of Granny grew by leaps and bounds. I knew this feisty little lady could do anything.

Granny proved to be the only stable thing in my dad's life, and almost every picture or story about him growing up involved her in some way. She was the ever-present glue that held everything together.

My dad was the pup of the family, and he remembered with great fondness growing up in the foothills of Missouri. He would hunt all kinds of animals, swim with the snakes in the rivers, and was content to just exist with nature.

However, the world was also a toxic place for my father. As a young boy, the years of living on the run took their toll. Dad lived one step ahead of the law, settling down wherever he could hide out—a shed he turned into a small house, a barn, or some other nondescript place.

One of his insecure homes caught fire and he lost all his earthly possessions. His rotten, haggard, and poor existence gave birth to a desperate desire for wealth, to a dream to rise above the poverty level. Into adulthood, his life became a constant search to improve his status, make a buck, and make it to the "big time."

Dad was the youngest of five kids, and his father impacted them all. Dan was the oldest child, and he grew up wild as a buck. The Nave blood flowed recklessly through him. He served time in prison and various jails and ended up paralyzed in a car accident. When I met Uncle Dan, he was living in our living room on an old hospital bed. His hands were permanently curved; the only movement he had was his arms and head. He was a fixture in our home, and life came to revolve around him. Granny was his nurse, adding to the faulty concept that she was some amazing medical miracle worker.

The next two children Granny had were girls, and then there was Uncle Joe. Uncle Joe stepped in when Dad was arrested. He was about the same height and build, and the same temperament boiled within him. One of the first stories I heard about Uncle Joe was of him walking down the street with Aunt Mona, his wife. A guy poked his head out of a pickup truck, made a lewd remark about Aunt Mona, and kept on driving. Seeing the guy stop at a red light, Uncle Joe ran after him, and the guy scrambled to roll up his window. Not to be outdone, Uncle Joe smashed his fist through the window, landing a blow to his face. The sacrifice of his hand was of no consequence in appeasing his anger.

Uncle Joe confided in me that he knew he would eventually come to a crossroads in life. He would have to either follow the downward trail of his Nave predecessors or fight to take the higher road. He chose to fight. Turning away from his evil trajectory and avoiding the criminal life, he went to work for GMC and also started buying and selling old houses. He showed me that it was possible to escape a criminal future, but that seemed incredibly boring to me.

Was the price of stability really worth it?

2: Dad's Early Years

My father grew up at my granny's side. She was his safe haven in his early teen years, as he strutted around like the perfect rebel—complete with his leather jacket collar up. He was cool, tough, and dripping with attitude. I had him pegged as the rebellious Fonzie from the TV show *Happy Days,* but he ended up more like the Marlon Brando image. Granny was also his safe haven when the flames ate up his few possessions and changed him inside, inspiring him to work hard to make a difference in this life.

My dad met my mother when she was a teenager and also having a tough go of it. My mother, Joyce, was the product of divorce. She was living with her mother and had an older stepsister and a younger baby brother. She bounced from home to home, dragged along with her mother's frequent moves. Her stepfather didn't want anything to do with her. That neglect made her the perfect target for my cool dad, who swept in and rescued her.

She started hanging out with this tough guy, feeling protected and clinging to the hope that he would take care of her and help her escape from her stepfather. Their love grew, and they eventually determined to seek a life of their own.

When her father found out about her rebel boyfriend, his anger drove him to the brink of insanity. The owner of a gas station in Peoria and a man of hard work and high ethics, he could see through my dad's hero veneer and knew that he was a bad seed. He did his best to tear their relationship apart, but the more he tried, the more resolved their determination to stay together became.

Eventually, the flame of his desire to separate them reached the end of their fuse and exploded into desperation. Dad, Mom, and their trusty sidekick Granny all took off and hid out in a shack in a gravel pit north of Detroit. Granny managed to forge a birth certificate for my mother, and around the age of sixteen or seventeen, my parents got legally—or should I say, illegally—hitched.

Mom got pregnant not long after their marriage, and along with the baby, the idea of a *Leave It to Beaver* family was born. Mom believed she had finally found her dream, and my dad had finally gotten his family. And Granny, well, she just became a mom to another child, soon to take on the caregiver role for my older brother.

Dad convinced Granny to purchase a gas station with him in Pontiac. She never could say no to my dad, and so the gas station was purchased, and Dad was officially on his way to earning that fortune that had always eluded him. However, the station did not work out as he had hoped, so he sold it and went to work doing this and that.

During the 1960s, working for one of the big three automakers was everyone's dream. Southeastern Michigan was the home of General Motors, Chrysler/Dodge, and Ford. The big three provided good wages and a healthy future. Dad wanted to be on his own but needed some source of income. And so, against his entrepreneurial nature, he signed on at GMC and went to work in the paint department, reluctantly trading in his life for the monotonous job of a factory worker.

His job was to climb a ladder and paint the hard-to-reach areas of the larger vehicles that were produced at the factory. It was a good, steady job, but it lacked what he needed—spice! Going to work every day, being a regular "Joe," and being stuck in a plant ate away at him, and he constantly thought about how to break out of the rut. This disease of will has impacted many of the members of my family line, and it continues to do so even today.

Eventually, he settled on the perfect plan for wealth development. While up on a ladder painting a large truck, he conveniently lost his footing and fell, landing under a doctor's care and quickly filing a lawsuit. If there were any suspicion that my dad had deliberately thrown himself off that ladder, nothing could be proven, and he received a large payoff. He used it to seed his potential empire, purchasing an apartment complex in Pontiac, Michigan, and setting about to become a real estate tycoon.

My oldest brother Jimmy was born around this time in 1961, and he brought great joy to my parents. But their lives were balancing on the edge of a volcano. The hopeful relationship my mom had dreamed about proved to be more fiction than fact, and she began to sense the evil side of my dad as soon as they ran off together.

She dug in and did her best to protect my brother, but my dad's dark side was growing, and she knew she had to escape. Dad was out like a dog in heat, looking for any woman who would hook up with him. His idea of faithfulness was that Mom would always be there for him. He, of course, lived under an entirely different set of rules. He was full of potential and driven, but Mom saw him as the angry man who would ruin her life.

She did the only thing she could. She took Jimmy and ran away with the help of her father, who had always been against my dad. My grandfather Irv hid them. Her escape was well orchestrated, but my father was not one to give up easily. He and Granny went to see a fortune-teller, who told them where Jimmy was being held. Dad and his accomplice drove to Kansas and kidnapped my brother without my mother's knowledge.

Just as they were getting Jimmy into the car, Mom noticed that he was gone and ran outside. Dad yelled out to her, "If you want to see your son, you had better get in the car!" That day marked the beginning of the end for my mother. She made the only decision she could. She would give up everything for the sake of her kid. That momentous decision would follow her as she eventually had three other boys. No matter what my father dragged her into, she couldn't let go of her children. It was an addiction of sorts. Running away again was out of the question because she would never abandon her children.

Mixed into this tale were my dad's distorted religious beliefs. Even though he was a rebel, deep down inside he craved a relationship with God. My granny had been exposed to the truth of Jesus Christ through the tireless work of a literature evangelist who came knocking on her door. She somehow scraped up enough money to buy a set of religious books that had been published by the Seventh-day Adventist Church, and as a result, she became a convert.

Granny resolved to raise her family with God, and so her five kids were all exposed to the Adventist Church. Three out of the five ended up joining, including my dad. He read the Bible, went through times of great faith, and then would have times of greater rebellion. He bounced back and forth between being the good son Abel and the bad son Cain, constantly fighting against himself.

3: Mom and Dad Try to Move Forward

My mom and dad got married, somehow survived the turbulent early years, and about the time my uncle helped my dad buy his first home in 1965, I was born.

I developed a nervous tic as a small child. The tension in my family was so high that my dad's family doctor said he had never seen a family like ours. He commented that if it were up to him, he would "medicate the whole bunch." A likely contribution to my disorder was a trip with Dad to the apartment complex he had purchased with the money from GMC. He drove us there amid gunfire and told us to stay down. Then he ran off and left us with no idea about what was going on. The stress of that night was indicative of life in the Nave household.

My dad eventually started to expand his fortune and went into business with my uncle Joe in a Corvette restoration shop. He would buy wrecked Corvettes, fix them up, and sell them for a profit. During this time, my one good childhood memory emerged. My dad bought a huge old bus and painted it green, and we spent about a month touring from Michigan to Missouri, riding in that big green bus. I think this is why one of my favorite movies today is the movie *RV*, with Robin Williams, because in it he rents a big green RV and tours with his family. And yes, perhaps it's a cheesy movie, but I like it nonetheless.

It didn't take too long for my dad and uncle to have a disagreement about the Corvette shop. A few years ago, my uncle told me that the reason the shop didn't work out was because Dad was always trying to rip him off. Uncle Joe had finally had enough, and they went their separate ways. Dad was on to other things to build his fortune. He would buy a house or a car, fix it up, and then sell it for a profit. If it was a house, we would live in it for a short time and then move out when it was ready to sell. It is hard to remember all the houses that came and went.

It seemed that Dad profited from whatever he touched, but it could never satisfy his innate desire for more. He bought an eighty-acre farm in Ortonville, Michigan, and a three hundred-acre ranch in Eldon, Missouri. Pretty soon his third child was born, Todd, and we seemed like the perfect little family.

I can remember time after time being complimented by people in church—yes, through it all, we were still faithful attendees at a local church—as to how well-behaved and cute we were. The perfect illusion of what a godly family should look like. People would compliment us week after week, having no idea what was really going on. My dad had mastered the façade, but on the inside, our family was a seething cauldron of dysfunction.

I can remember having to sit perfectly still in church. If we giggled or got out of control, we were pinched, and it always seemed that when we got home from church, we were spanked because we just could not behave. I can remember one stretch of time where we would come home from church and I would run to my room and kneel down at my bed to pray because I knew that my father would not spank me if I was praying. That tactic worked only for so long, however, and soon even prayer did not stop his wrath.

Dad had a raging temper and a bit of a control problem to boot. Early on, he would discipline us by striking our bare skin with a horse whip, causing welts and bruises. If we ever touched someone else's vehicle, we would be whipped with a belt. We were taught to respect everyone, and if we ever showed any disrespect, we would be punished. Now, disrespect was defined by my father's mood, so it was a thing not easily defined. We would get beaten for talking back, laughing at the dinner table, being a minute late for some appointment, or for any reason that seemed remotely feasible at the moment.

We would sit at the dinner table, and no one would breathe until we identified Dad's mood. He had ice-blue eyes that completely masked his demeanor, making it impossible to tell whether he was aggravated or in a good state of mind. We walked on eggshells, as he was always on the cusp of exploding.

But as bad as my dad's behavior was, there was another thing that slipped into our home that was even worse. By the age of five, I had been sexually molested, and for years I went through life being abused by various people who had access to our home. I was so starved for love that anyone wanting to hold me was rewarded with whatever behavior they requested.

It has taken me years to put this down on paper because I haven't wanted to acknowledge all the ugliness that has happened to me. If you have ever been abused, you know the pain, guilt, and shame that come with abuse. I still struggle with the effects of those years, and whenever I see a little kid, I can't help but think how sick someone would have to be to abuse a child.

I knew a great deal about sex by the ripe old age of five and had already learned to disassociate who I was from what happened to me. My body was physically and sexually abused, but I refused to let my mind accept it. I have more memories with my clothes off than on at that age, and as a result, I developed a false sense of sexuality. To me, sex was dirty and shameful.

All I wanted was for someone to accept and love me. I longed for someone to be proud of me—especially my father—but he was too busy with everyone else. It all came to a head in the spring of 1974, when I was eight years old and we were living on the eighty-acre farm in Ortonville, Michigan. I woke up one morning and my father was gone. He had disappeared in the night, and I blamed myself. I had gone to bed the night before without giving him a kiss and a hug because I was mad at him. Now my eight-year-old mind was racked with guilt.

No one spoke of his whereabouts for months, and the tension in our home reached a new high. My mind played and replayed all the scenarios as to why my dad would leave me, and my ache grew daily.

Four months later, my cousin secretly told me that my dad had been arrested on the charge of first-degree murder. I was in shock. He was accused of killing two men in a drug deal that had gone sour near Port Huron, Michigan. I could not believe that my dad could have done something that horrible, and I remember sitting behind him in the courtroom later trying to understand how anyone could think that he had done anything wrong.

4: Prison

As the court proceedings dragged on, all our money went to lawyers, and we ended up broke and had to move in with our aunt and uncle in Drayton Plains. Part of the reason we ended up living there was that everyone was afraid that someone was going to seek revenge against my dad and attack us. The last few days that we lived on the farm in Ortonville, my uncle Joe came out and made a barbed-wire gate so people couldn't drive up freely to our house.

We had lost our home and were now all crowded into a small bedroom, unsure as to what was going on. We ended up on welfare, and each time we paid for groceries with coupons from a booklet, I felt as if everyone in the store was looking at me and talking about "that poor little kid." I hated being poor, having a dad in prison, having to rely on others, and watching my mom in her agony.

I eventually learned what my dad had really done when I was searching his name on the Internet just a few years ago. In an article written by the prosecuting attorney in St. Clair County at that time, I discovered that my father and two other men had robbed an isolated home in the country in an attempt to steal a large sum of money from drug dealers. When the deal went sour, the drug dealers were killed and my dad and his two friends burned the house down to eliminate any evidence. While running from the house, one of my dad's friends, an outlaw biker who went by the name of Jesus, was shot twice. My dad and his other friend left him for dead in a field. When captured, this biker helped finger my dad, which led to his arrest. On the day of the trial, my dad and the other man who had committed this crime took a plea deal, pleading guilty to second-degree murder. As a result, my father was given a sentence of ten to twenty years.

He was sent away to the Jackson State Penitentiary in Jackson, Michigan, and we began the humiliating, weekly ritual of driving from Pontiac to Jackson to visit him. I can still retrace the steps in my mind. We would get on the interstate and drive by Ann Arbor, where I imagined I would attend the University of Michigan one day. But instead of taking an exit there, we took the Jackson exit, where signs were posted warning people to avoid hitchhikers because a prison was nearby.

After driving through the worst part of the city, a huge, red brick building would eventually emerge. It was surrounded by a high fence with rolls of razor wire at the top and bottom. Large guard towers looming high in the sky looked down at us as we drove up to the entrance flanked by armed guards. One of them would ask why we were there, and we would recite my father's prison number, which still rots in my brain to this day—141154.

As we went through the large prison doors, we entered a sterile world of raw chaos. Vending machines lined the walls, hard plastic chairs with multicolored gum stuck to them dotted a landscape where hundreds of people loitered, children jumped and ran around out of control, and babies screamed. On the other side of this surreal scene was a wall of lockers and a place to check in.

We were given a locker key with a large, silver metal piece attached. We were instructed to place all of our belongings into that locker so that we would not have anything with us in the prison waiting room. We obeyed and began the wait that often lasted for hours for our short visit with our dad. At the end of eternity, our name was called and we lined up like sheep led to the slaughter to be ushered through the metal detector. We were searched, but it felt more like being assaulted. Any dignity we had left was tossed out the window, and fear spun out of control in our guts. The first set of iron bars opened, we stepped in, and they clanged shut behind us, echoing down the hallway and right into our souls.

Now we were trapped, with bars behind us and bars ahead of us. Even though we had done nothing wrong, we felt like new felons arriving. Armed guards grimaced at us from behind the glass of a large room off to the side. We approached a seated guard who dipped what looked like a large cotton swab in some clear liquid and made a big, cold mark on the backside of our hands. This was important because on our way out, when we put our hands under an ultraviolet light, if the purple mark did not appear, we would not be allowed to leave. I remember being terrified that mine would somehow get wiped off and I would be stuck behind those prison bars for the rest of my life.

Another set of bars opened, leading to a big, steel door. We were herded through this doorway into a large visiting room with cameras and guards everywhere. After being warned to behave, we would find a place to squeeze between other people in chairs arranged in semicircles.

A door would buzz, and our dad would walk in and look around for us. When he spotted us, he would smile and walk over. We were not allowed to make any sudden movements, so instead of attacking him with hugs, we had to embrace him slowly and quietly. He would sit down with us, and we would take turns sitting next to him, all the while feeling the stares of others, of the guards, and of the cameras. My blood pressure always felt like it soared to record highs.

My older brother described one aspect of the effects of our prison visits. Our understanding of the good guys got distorted; we began seeing the police as the bad guys and the criminals as the innocent victims. Visiting Dad in prison, being on welfare, and being abused all mixed together, creating a hateful venom that began to boil within me and would brew for many years.

5: Tug-of-War

With emotional poison racing through my veins, I eased the ache by trying to get my dad out of prison. I wrote President Jimmy Carter and begged him to intervene, assuring him that my dad was an innocent man. I never heard back, but that didn't stop me from writing to the governor. My mother also petitioned government officials, but no one was open to our cries of innocence—likely because my dad had pled guilty. I had no idea that he had admitted to the crime.

We were attending the Holly Seventh-day Adventist Church at the time, and as we sunk deeper into destitution, the church stepped in to help us. Somehow, they had acquired an old house and offered us a great deal on renting it. We moved in, and the church continued providing for many of our needs.

It was during our time in Holly that several good things happened. Several godly men from that church began to help us fill the emotional void deep within us. Mr. Chamberlain, a retired man and a member of the church, became the caretaker of the property and became like a grandfather to us. He was always fixing something on the property and would encourage us as best he could. Rick Sutton was another man who impacted our lives. Rick ran a local gas station, and he befriended us and served as a father figure to us four small boys, wrestling with us on many occasions. The pastor of the Holly church, Pastor Earl Zager, was incredible as well. He devoted himself to pouring God's love into us and made a deep positive impact on our family. The years we spent in Holly were the ones in which we got to see the good of what a church could do.

But evil tagged along behind the good. The sexual abuse continued in my life, and in addition, my Christian classmates teased me mercilessly. Many times I would be walking home from school with kids on the other side of the street screaming that I was a loser because my dad was in prison. Once again, even though I had not done anything wrong, I felt as though I was the one being punished. I felt that I was evil and damned.

I tried to escape by smoking cigarettes and engaging in petty theft. I would steal a pack of cigarettes from the grocery store and then hide in a wooded area near the house. As I "smoked" (not knowing I was supposed to inhale), I knew I was doing wrong, but I also felt I was living as I truly felt. An evil person should do evil things.

I struggled with guilt, shame, fear, anger, and pretty much every emotion possible. My identity was forming, and it was not looking promising. As the battle between good and evil for my soul raged within me, a new soldier appeared at the front lines. A church youth leader began to really encourage me. He even had a woman from the church buy me a new backpack and was going to take me, along with several other boys, on a campout to an island off Michigan's Upper Peninsula. For a brief moment, I felt special. Excitement and pride burst at my seams as I packed that backpack for the trip.

Then—a sucker punch.

6: The Great Escape

For years we went to visit my dad almost weekly. His transfer to a minimum security prison vastly improved the atmosphere of our visits, and the sound of clanging metal bars and the humiliation of being searched by prison guards became a normal part of life.

It doesn't take long to be conditioned to the victim role. As a small child, I had been "marked" as a troublemaker because of my dad. People joked about our last name, and people saw us as those "no good" kids. I had been teased, bullied, beaten, and abused, and when I added in the humiliation that went along with visiting my dad in prison, I was sure I was worthless and had no hope for a good future. I can still feel the incredible sense of deep loss of identity and value.

When my dad was sent away, my mother gave birth to her youngest child, nine years my junior. And so we would haul Jason around wherever we went.

When my dad was transferred to the low-level security prison, something changed inside of him and a plan was hatched. It was the fall of 1977. School had just begun, and I had entered the seventh grade. I had also been selected to serve as a junior deacon at my church. My father chose this particular moment to escape from prison.

My brothers and I did not know it at the time, but our lives were about to be forever scarred in a way that no one could ever imagine. Up until that point, I didn't think anything worse could happen. We had no stability, we were seen as worthless kids, and our friends were eventually told to leave us alone. We seemed to have some sort of evil letter carved on our foreheads, and we were as low as we could get. Bad thing after bad thing happened, and every time a small sliver of hope appeared, it was blacked out in some dramatic way. It was as if Satan was telling me that I could never escape, that there was never going to be anything good for me. My life was doomed to be one of tragic pain and suffering, and I could only imagine what the end would look like.

I was getting ready to go camping with some people from church and had just packed my new backpack. But my mom told me I couldn't go because we were going camping somewhere else and to get the station wagon loaded. She also told me I couldn't take my new backpack with me. Several relatives came to visit, and Mom began acting very strangely. She talked quietly with these people she didn't really like about something we kids didn't know anything about. When they left, we continued with our camping plans.

We all piled into the station wagon and drove to a wooded area near Dad's prison. I was thinking how strange it was to be camping there, when Mom started telling us to look for Dad. I had no idea what she was talking about because Dad was in prison, living in some cabin behind a tall fence. But Mom was resolute in her instructions, and so we started looking out the windows for Dad.

We drove by the prison property once and didn't see anything. As Mom turned around and drove back toward the prison, and I began to believe that Mom was losing it, my father appeared right before my eyes. He was with another guy (we would learn later that his name was Burt), and they were running down a hillside carrying two large duffel bags. The brakes screeched as Mom stopped the car, Dad and the other man squeezed in, and like a big rolling can of sardines, we were off.

No one said a word, and I was pretty sure I wasn't breathing. Mom drove and drove and drove in a completely silent car. Eventually, it got dark, and she just kept driving. I had no idea what direction we were headed until a sign rolled past my window that said "Welcome to Indiana."

Mom finally slowed the car and pulled into the parking lot of a twenty-four-hour restaurant. We all packed into a booth and started nervously eating when a group of police officers walked in. As they walked past us to their table, the temperature shot up about a thousand degrees, and I crammed down my fear of a shoot-out by staring at my food and reminding myself to swallow.

We managed to slip out of the restaurant in one piece and drove farther into Indiana, finding ourselves driving around a large cemetery. It was dark, foggy, and all around us were headstones and graves. My nerves were shot, and I just knew we were going to die in the cemetery—either by the police or by a zombie. We stayed there for a long time until an alarm clock rang in my dad's head, and he announced it was time to go. I learned later that it was not a cemetery but a monastery. All I remembered were gargoyles and vampires.

Back in the car, we drove deeper into the night, arriving at an old, single-story motel. Inside our room we were introduced to Burt's family, who had driven there to meet us, and to another man who looked strangely similar to my dad. That man's last name was Kulwicki, and when they swapped driver's licenses, my dad instructed us that our last name was now Kulwicki.

I remember practicing the spelling of my new last name because I was afraid that if we got stopped and I was asked to spell it, I would crack under the pressure and be responsible for sending my dad back to prison. I tried to make up a song for it but didn't do very well, because of my shattered nerves.

For the next three months, we alternated between sleeping in a tent and in the car in Greeley, Colorado. We had lost our home, our identities, and we were constantly being told not to make any friends or even talk to anyone. I would like to say that this time was exciting, but terrifying is a more appropriate word as we lived every day in fear of being discovered. Questions pelted me constantly. What if someone asked my name and I slipped and said, "Nave"? What if I froze when confronted by a police officer? Would I be shot? Was I now a criminal?

We slowly worked our way across the United States until we reached Nevada. When we arrived in Las Vegas, we rented a tiny apartment with the other family that had escaped, and we attempted to survive. There was monumental tension with all of us packed into that two-bedroom mini-apartment. We kids couldn't go outside much, could not to talk to anyone, and certainly could not make friends, so our little apartment became our prison.

We had been locked away in this "prison cell" for a few weeks when my dad and Burt managed to find a twenty-seven-foot travel trailer that had rolled over and was in need of repair. They purchased it and began to fix it up little by little. When it was completed—minus the bathroom—my dad moved us into a casino trailer park in North Las Vegas. Dad informed us that once again our name was going to change. This time we went from Kulwicki to Dumke, and right away I hated it. Dumke was too close to "donkey."

We enrolled in a large inner-city Vegas school, and the very first day a guy beat me up for simply being a white kid in a mostly black school. It was agonizing going to that school, and each day I thought I was going to be killed. I was teased, threatened, and my books were constantly being stolen. Eventually, one black kid stood up for me and I was able to relax a bit as long as I was around him.

My oldest brother got a job at McDonald's, and we would anxiously await his arrival from work because he would bring with him the food that was thrown out by McDonald's and we would eat it. This worked great until the night we all got food poisoning. I will never forget how quickly one's stomach can be emptied.

We stayed in Vegas a few more months until my dad and Burt decided that they needed to separate—I guess to improve their odds of staying on the lamb. Burt chose California, and so my dad chose to head the other way. Among the many reasons I was glad to leave was the chance to get away from a deviant guy that Dad had befriended who went out of his way to abuse kids. Dad was unaware of this, and we sure weren't going to tell anyone.

7: Moving to Florida

When January 1978 rolled around, we packed up our travel trailer and left Vegas, bound for Miami, Florida. The trip took about a month and was an experience in supernatural preservation. A trailer came off its hitch right in front of us, barely missing us as it weaved off the road. An axle snapped in Needles, California. We broke down on the Sunshine Skyway in Tampa—probably the scariest bridge I have ever seen in my life. And we somehow survived being cramped up with each other through some extreme weather.

Reflecting on that trip, it really seems like a nightmare. We were living on the run, we had no money, and each time a police car passed, my heart would jump out of my throat. We were trying to be average people in a very nonaverage way. Lies had encapsulated each one of us, and we were forced to appear as the perfect family. My youngest brother, Jason, had no idea that Dumke wasn't his real last name because he was just too little to understand. To him, our crazy life was normal.

My feet started to outgrow my tennis shoes, a cheap version of the blue-and-white ones inspired by the TV show *Starsky & Hutch*. We couldn't afford new shoes, so I took a knife and cut out a hole for my toe to stick out. Then the side of the shoes went, and I had to cut some more. Eventually, it took tape and a lot of luck to keep my shoes on my feet at all.

We drove into Florida excited because we had the feeling that we were finally settling down. Drifting down the western side of the state, we stopped in Bonita Springs and parked our little trailer in a deserted place by the water. I remember seeing huge blue crabs walking up on the beach. That was creepy. Every night I would go outside, look up at the stars, and imagine I was free. Sadly, the next day returned me to the prison cell of my life. Trying to live a normal life was tough, and I could see the toll that living on the run was taking on all of us.

Dad had gotten a job putting up billboard advertisements, which had brought in some much-needed money. But soon the job didn't work out and we were back on the road, this time headed for Miami. My dad thought that Miami was a good place to get lost, and my mom's mother and stepfather lived there.

When we arrived in Miami, we settled into a trailer park in a section of Miami called Sweetwater, right off Flagler Street. Since we planned to stay a while, I was enrolled in the W. R. Thomas Jr. High School, and my brothers went to their respective schools, as well.

My father, who now went by the name Bill Dumke, got a job as a body shop foreman at a Ford dealership, and life seemed to be as normal as it could be under the circumstances. Our main way of surviving was to stay out of the trailer for as long as we could. Florida weather was fairly temperate, and we just tried to enjoy being outside as much as possible.

My father enforced very strict rules with an iron fist. We could not tell anyone anything about our past. We could not talk about our parents or where we were from. We could never make contact with anyone who was a relative. No one was allowed into our living space, and we were not allowed to go into anyone else's living space. We were expected to be model citizens so as not to arouse unnecessary attention. We also had to keep our windows closed, with blinds drawn *at all times,* and we were instructed to never answer the phone.

Dad was a mini-Hitler. I used to defend his actions saying that he needed to do what he did to protect us, but as I grew older, I realized that everything my father did during this time was selfish—ripping us out of school, dragging us around the United States, teaching us to lie, hide, and never tell anything to anyone, and constantly drilling into us that the law and the police were evil.

I don't know exactly how, but we survived our first few months in Miami, and I managed to finish the seventh grade. When summer came, Dad rewarded us by moving us into a single-wide mobile home in the same trailer park. It was like winning the lottery! Now we could move around, we had a nice toilet—actually two toilets—we had a shower, and we had a big refrigerator that actually worked. We had finally made it to the big time! We parked our little travel trailer next to our new home; it was a visual illustration of our moving up in the world.

About this time, my dad became friends with an insurance guy who was as crooked as he could be. Vince introduced Dad to the organized crime scene in South Florida, which during the late seventies and early eighties was a drug dealer's dream come true. Vince was from Cuba and had ties to all sorts of shady characters, who soon took a liking to my father.

It didn't take long for my dad to quit his job at the Ford dealership and start working for one of these shady characters, Alfredo, who ran a mob furniture store. Dad got promoted to an auto body repair facility, where I also got to work. He moved on up the mob corporate ladder, settling into his new position as a bodyguard, or enforcer, for Alfredo. Wherever Alfredo went, my dad went. It was this last promotion that set up my father for a life of high criminal activity.

Alfredo was a ruthless drug dealer and had no patience for anyone who would get in his way. He was busy building an empire, and during the great Miami riots of 1980, my dad was Alfredo's bodyguard as he ventured through the tragedy that came to be known as Little Havana. Hundreds were killed and thousands injured as the National Guard was called in to restore order. Alfredo thrived during this time, and as he became more influential, so did my father.

As my father continued up the criminal stairway, it became all too clear what he was capable of doing. He started carrying guns and knives, drinking heavily, and using drugs. Acquiring the nickname "Peter Rabbit," he would come home with a briefcase full of money almost every night. He would call upon me to count it, and as millions of dollars passed through my fingers, I desperately wished just a little of it were mine. But I knew that if I took a single dollar, it would cost me my life.

In a few short years, my dad had worked his way up to being a drug dealer. He worked alongside several drug dealers who didn't like each other, but they all liked my dad. As a result, he made more and more connections. He worked for Alfredo, for Bud the Hillbilly, and for Little. I often traveled with him, and he would constantly remind me not to say anything about a dealer to another dealer. I was to keep my mouth shut, and I learned early on to zip my lip and just observe.

I learned from Bud how to launder drug money through pig farming. The pig stench was an appropriate cover for what was transpiring. With Alfredo, I learned about running crooked businesses, laundering money through other avenues, and the power of intimidation. I often hung out with one of Alfredo's guys, Rafael, whose sole job was to mix creative explosive concoctions used to intimidate those who chose to oppose Alfredo's growing empire.

Little was the strangest of the bunch. He was very guarded and kept himself out of sight much of the time. He ran things from his large house on the outskirts of Miami, and when Dad took me there, he would position me in the horse barn near the feed. Placing a MAC-10 machine gun next to me, he told me that if I saw anyone moving in the field behind the house, I should start firing as fast as I could.

I felt like Clint Eastwood in one of his Spaghetti Westerns, and I felt very important. The tingle of the power I felt while holding that gun meant I could dictate the future around me. I learned what fear was all about and how to channel that fear into control and power. I also learned how it felt to live under the constant threat of death. I was hanging around my dad's friends more and more, and as many of them got murdered, I realized that something bad could happen to me at any time. I must always be on guard.

Whether driving like madmen through the mountains of North Carolina transporting illegal substances and hoping to not get caught, or running drugs in Miami, I hung around with murderers, thieves, drug dealers, and beautiful women who were after only one thing—power. It was a surreal life and one that I would find myself enjoying more and more. It was a nervous, anxious, and dangerous way to live, as many who tried their hand in this field either got killed or arrested. Most had a short life span, but the few who were somehow able to navigate it lived lives of luxury. The game had worse odds than the lottery, but I thought I was clever enough to play and win—to escape the law. A plan for my future was hatched—a plan that involved making enough money to have anything I ever wanted.

8: The Potential Drug Dealer

As the equivalent of my godfather, Bud took me under his wing. He would give me aspirin containers full of pure cocaine. By the time I was sixteen years of age, I was driving a stolen car, carrying a knife in my boot, talking with an attitude, drinking large quantities of vodka just to start my day, and life started losing its interest. I also had lost all sense of fear and pretty much felt as though I was invincible.

Bud introduced me to many influential people. One man was a hit man for the mob—at nineteen years old. That meant his job was to eliminate people who were "in the way." I asked him about his trade, and he told me he carried only a single-shot rifle. I told him that was pretty stupid, in the event that he missed. He replied that he never missed. I thought that was pretty cool, and so I added "hit man" to my list of possible careers.

Bud had a falling-out with my dad over Dad's growing greed and lust. Bud told me that my dad would chase any skirt who had a lot of money and that my dad was addicted to money and power. Bud offered to help me in spite of my dad, telling me I could do whatever I wanted and that he would support me. I became Bud's football analyst and told him who would win what football games. I won a large sum of money for him, and he paid me with decent cash, a custom knife, and a very nice Winchester .30-30 rifle (pre–1964). He loved me like a son, and I would later use that connection to my advantage.

Meanwhile, my father was rapidly rising in the ranks of organized crime, getting in with the Cuban and Haitian refugees coming into Miami. He used to joke about being part of the "cocaine cowboys," a term that was designated for those who defended the illegal drug trade with reckless abandon. In fact, a documentary called *Cocaine Cowboys* was produced about this time, but even it doesn't do justice to the times of South Florida during this stretch of history.

The city was a hodgepodge of drug and gang wars, and when you turned on the news, you could see people from Haiti arriving on the beach in boats and running for freedom. Little Havana was a section of Miami that was especially volatile. Many had escaped from Fidel Castro's clutches, and they did not want to be taken advantage of again. Castro had cleaned out his prisons and had sent many of the deranged people over to the United States via boats. When they arrived in Miami, these people were rounded up and placed in a large fenced-in camp underneath the expressway that became their home away from home. We would drive over that section of the highway and see this huge tent city below us, imagining the terrible things that were being done there.

During this time, my crazy father got drunk, walked into the Cuban radio station, held the radio host at gunpoint, and proclaimed a message of freedom for the masses—even though he couldn't speak Spanish. I didn't expect my father to return from that trip, but he had no fear and, somehow, people respected him.

My father used to brag about the people he had killed, the women he had slept with, and the deals he had made. As a result of my dad's way of life, my older brother became a nervous wreck and went up to Michigan to live with Granny. Left alone to hold everything together, I fell in love with making everything work. I was indeed the savior of my family, and I sought to keep everyone safe and secure. I stepped into the dad role for my youngest brother and tried to balance life and my desire to make it on my own.

Drugs and alcohol were the main way we all stayed "sane" during this time. We had great access to both, and there was not a day we were not aware that someone could be out tracking us. It could have been the government hunting for my dad, drug dealers trying to get revenge, or someone else trying to muscle their way up the ranks of unorganized crime. We were taught to fear the police, and as a result, they became the "bad guys" to us, and the criminals were the misunderstood "good guys."

One time, my dad and I were out working on a car one day when some ducks flew overhead. I yelled out to my dad, "Duck!" He hit the ground, thinking someone was getting ready to shoot at him. I had never seen anyone move so fast! Another time, we were driving a big Lincoln down the interstate, dodging cars and trying to escape someone chasing us. The tension was palpable and always surrounded us.

Dad was part of a crew that would walk through the Everglades picking up drugs that pilots flying back from South America had dropped out of the sky. I think this was when my fear of alligators began. I knew there were alligator nests under the water, but someone had told me that a gator could grab you and drag you down into its underground bunker while you were still alive. I was never sure if this was true or not, but it planted seeds of fear regardless.

During my ninth-grade year, I had managed to learn the majority of Spanish cuss words and was enjoying my time of hanging out with drug dealers and drinking the official "soft drink" of South Miami—Michelob beer.

Gangs had infiltrated the junior high school I attended, and I was invited to join one. From my perspective, the school gangs were not as powerful as the adult versions, so I turned the invitation down and hung out with my dad instead. I went to school, worked with my dad, and sunk deeper and deeper into the drug culture.

I also started hanging out with Freddy, Bud's son, and we developed our own little ritual. We would start out by drinking a couple of Stroh's beers, then some German beer, and then we would break out the cocaine and tequila. I can remember attempting to drive home from Hialeah to Miami after one such adventure and having the highway disappear and reappear. The powerful effects of cocaine and alcohol really warped my sense of reality, and many times I cheated death through some strange concoction.

While under the influence, I did many stupid things. I would drive like a maniac, spin the car in circles at the intersection, challenge anyone around me, and walk up to people holding guns and grab them out of their hands. I even got into a few fights where I would black out with rage and then all of a sudden snap out of it.

As my dad's tenure in the South Miami crime zone increased, so did mine. I was making connections with the movers and shakers, meeting judges and politicians, and in my mind was planning my rise to the top. I would hang out at Bud's townhouse, where it was pretty much a party that never ended. The huge television covering the wall was always showing some movie, there were refreshments of various types everywhere, and garbage was tossed here and there. People would come in, flop down for a bit, and then head back out. When you sat down, you had to make sure that you were not sitting on someone's gun or flirting with someone's girlfriend for the day or night.

I drove around from gravel pits to pig farms to stores that served as fronts for some criminal element, or out to some mansion to meet with strange people with even stranger methods of conducting business. There was always someone who had just gotten shot or who had been killed, and the corruption of the times ran rampant. I think that if you were to look up the statistics for Dade County during this time, you would see the excess of crime. Dade County became the joke of the nation and even made the cover of *Time* magazine.

During the heyday of the drug wars, a group of FBI agents were gunned down outside of a bank, and the drug dealers had no fear of any authority. My dad and I watched the TV news coverage of the massacre and laughed while we told ourselves, "They deserved it." There were more crooked cops than honest ones, politicians were corrupt, senators had been bought, and if you weren't involved in something illegal, you were seen as the strange one.

My dad sank deeper and deeper into this scene. While he was freebasing cocaine, many nights he would overdose and my mom and I would have to walk him around the house holding ice cubes on his wrists and forehead to keep him alive. I thought he was a goner many times, but he was a tough old bird and always bounced back.

Now, one of the few benefits of having a drug dealer for a father was that word soon drifted out to the neighborhood and no one messed with me; everyone feared my father. One time, a neighbor was yelling at my brother in the little neighborhood park. When my mom went out to try to ease the situation, the man turned on my mother and started screaming at her. It was more than my dad could take. He burst out of the door, stalked up to the man, stood up as tall as he could, and got in the guy's face. Still not backing down, the man snapped, "What are you going to do, kill me?" My dad, with rage tattooed on his face, growled through clenched teeth, "That can be arranged, sport." As the man panicked and disappeared into his house, I stuck my chest out and let everyone know that my dad could take their dad any day!

9: Extradited

Near the end of my tenth-grade year, the FBI finally tracked my father down. Using a silent campaign, they evacuated a large part of the trailer park and had the manager of the park call my mother so she would come up to the office. With me and my two brothers at school, they knew my dad was alone in the trailer.

As my mother walked toward the office, she began to feel uneasy. When it dawned on her what was happening, she turned and dashed back to warn Dad—but it was too late. She ran right into two federal agents. As they approached the trailer, they informed my dad that he was surrounded and that he should come out unarmed with his hands in the air. Dad entertained the thought of going out firing, but they had caught him in one of his hungover, sane, melancholy moments, so he actually did what they asked. Hiding some money and guns under the bed, he just got up and walked out. The cops converged, and after years of living on the run, my dad was now officially captured.

The drama moved quickly, and as soon as my dad was removed from the premises, the quarantine was lifted and people came back into the area. When I got home from track practice a few hours later, things seemed a little too quiet; something just didn't seem right. I carefully parked my bike, walked slowly into our trailer, and looked around. No one was home. I wasn't surprised that my brothers weren't home, but where was my mom? When I entered the kitchen, my eyes rested on a business card on the kitchen table from an FBI agent named Donahue. I surmised that either my dad had been caught or that he was on the run again. Were we now on our own in Miami? Had Mom and Dad taken off and left me in charge? I hadn't talked to a relative in a long time, and there was no way I was going to place a call to the police to ask what had happened, so I was left with that choice that no one likes—waiting.

Eventually, Mom returned and told me that Dad had been arrested and transported to the Miami city jail. He had been arrested for fleeing the State of Michigan and for escaping from prison. But strangely, he was never charged with anything else because the Feds were apparently convinced he had become a good, all-American pig farmer!

Over the next few months, my father made several court appearances dressed in a bright orange jumpsuit. We visited him weekly in the Dade County jail, which took us back to those Jackson Prison days. This time, we sat in a small space and talked to Dad through a heavy mesh grate at the bottom of a window. It was not the best, but it was all that was allowed.

During our visits, Dad told me to be on the alert because some people might be coming to the house to ask some questions. Sure enough, just a few days later when I got home from school, a plain brown car pulled up in front of the trailer and two guys got out. They were both wearing suits and looked like police officers at first. But if they were police officers, the look in their eyes made me think they were probably crooked.

I tried to ignore them, but they followed me into our fenced-in yard and shut the gate behind them. They positioned themselves between me and the door to our trailer, and one of them pulled back his jacket to show the gun tucked into his belt. My uneasiness grew as they grilled me about the whereabouts of Bill Dumke—who, of course, was also Jim Nave. Panicking, I tried to lie my way out, but I was not doing a good job at all. They started inching toward me, and I tried to brace myself for what was about to take place. Just before they reached me, the older lady living behind us stormed out of her trailer and started yelling at them.

Thrown off of their plan, they cussed her out, threatened her, and then sharply announced that they would be back. Terrified, I managed to scramble up the stairs to our trailer and get inside just as they were leaving. My mouth fell open in absolute shock when I got inside. There were my mom and brothers all hunkered down—hiding! I could hardly believe that my mom had left me to hang.

Life continued onward with my dad in jail and me thinking that each time I went home someone was going to jump me. I started taking different routes home to make sure I wasn't being followed. I figured that Dad owed some guys some money or something, and I knew that he had come up with at least twenty thousand dollars from somewhere and hidden it under the bed.

Eventually, my dad was extradited back to Michigan. The summer had passed, and we learned that Dad was going back to Jackson State Prison. I couldn't believe it. The place he had escaped from was now his destination. So they took him away, shackled head to toe, in a small plane that hit about every storm possible before crashing. My dad later told me that he was sure they were all going to die because of the storm.

While he was gone, my mother, two younger brothers, and I coped the best we could. We had no income, but my dad had kept the briefcase with the twenty thousand dollars under the bed, so we were not in deep need at the moment. Eventually, I decided that I wanted to be closer to my dad, so I moved to Michigan and ended up living with Granny. I got a job at a local pizza restaurant and enrolled in the eleventh grade at Pontiac Northern Senior High School.

It was a tough transition going from the world of crime to one where Granny tried to bring me up right. I now had rules, no money, and was stuck in a climate that got very cold. As I worked cleaning tables at the pizza place, I kept thinking how much I could be making if I were back in Miami. What a waste of time! I could not see how anyone would want to be legit because there sure didn't seem to be much money in it.

At school, four kids came up behind me and hit me with brass knuckles. I was out of school for a month healing from a broken jaw. Of course, they couldn't put a cast on my jaw, but they could wire my mouth shut so that it would heal in place. After the procedure, the doctor told me to always carry a pair of wire cutters, because if I got sick and threw up, I would drown—such a pleasant thought.

I managed to finish off my classes with the school's help, but the hatred in me had risen to a new high. Now it was my health that was being impacted, and I was mad. My cousin and I went out looking for the guys who broke my jaw. Taking a rifle and pistol along with us, we would have killed them if we had found them. There was only hatred in my heart and I wanted revenge.

We spent the day hunting for them, but didn't find them. I had to settle for thoughts of doing them harm, but it wasn't enough. Any sparkle in my eyes had been replaced by a dull evil that just wouldn't go away. I didn't fully comprehend that this was an outgrowth of the life of hatred and crime that had permeated my family history.

10: The Heritage

Even though I had witnessed the powerful negative effects of a life of crime in my own immediate family and knew about my family's heritage, it wasn't until I was an adult that I did some genealogical research and discovered, much to my chagrin, the full picture. We were directly related to Jesse James, who roamed the hills of Missouri around the time of the Civil War. Jesse's dad was a preacher who tried to keep his son on the straight and narrow, but Jesse, with his wild hair and lifestyle, made the decision to ride with those who stood against President Lincoln and the Northerners.

When the state of Missouri had to choose between allegiance to the North or the South, it was leaning toward the South. Not wanting to lose the state, President Lincoln convinced the immigrants in St. Louis to vote and support the North—and they did. The contingent from St. Louis voted for the North, and the rest of the state went South, causing a state civil war. President Lincoln gave the order that he would allow whatever had to be done to convince the rest of the state to side with the North. History tells us that Northern troops would gather up women and children and burn them alive to convince their husbands and fathers to help the North. However, instead of turning the hearts toward the North, the men became all the more determined to overthrow it. Jesse James rode with one such man, William Contrell.

It was a bloody time, and one of the bloodthirstiest men of that era was Jim Nave, a man with the same name as my father. Jim murdered, pillaged, and sought revenge against the North. When he was caught and sentenced to die, he escaped, but then was caught again and killed. The similarities between him and my dad were eerie. Distrust in government ran deep in our bones, and that heritage of crime and mistrust only grew through the years.

Unfortunately, it wasn't only in the Missouri area that our lineage was linked to a life of crime. We were also related to one of the members of the ruthless Purple Gang in Detroit—the only gang that Al Capone feared. We also had family members in organized crime through the mafia in Detroit. My dad used to drive me by the place that Jimmy Hoffa had disappeared, and I was taught that the unions were as ruthless as could be.

Many of my relatives worked on the wrong side of the police force, and the stories that I soaked up had me thinking that I was born to be an outlaw. I knew that the majority of the men in our family had done time in jail or prison, but I truly felt I was smarter than the average Joe. I would spend my time thinking, pondering, analyzing, and figuring out ways to make the organized crime life pay and eliminate the risk of being caught. My favorite scenario involved robbing a bank. I had the plan figured out but never got the chance to attempt it, which in hindsight I realize was due only to the grace of God.

By Christmas break, some three months after I had moved to Michigan to be closer to my dad, I had had enough of the straight life and was determined to make my mark. I got in touch with Bud back in Miami and started helping him again bet on various sporting events. I also got in touch with my dad's friend Vince and set up a cocaine buy and sell. I even managed to purchase a large truckload of marijuana coming from the West Coast. Busy wheeling and dealing, I bought airline tickets and flew from Detroit to Miami without my grandmother knowing. I was tired of the "good life" and wanted to get back in the game.

When I arrived in Miami, I was greeted by a friend, Carlos, who was driving a new Cadillac. I wasted no time setting the plan into full motion and enjoying the finer things of Miami, as well. I drove his Caddy, ate the finest food, and purchased the best coke I could find. I rented a couple of rooms at a hotel and partied as often as I could.

I had brought my dad's hotbox to Miami, a small wooden electronic device resembling a case that held a fifth of whiskey. Inside was an LED display and a place to put a sample of cocaine where it would be heated up and measured for purity. Just having one guaranteed jail time, but it was a necessary part of big-time drug deals, eliminating the possibility of purchasing cut drugs, which would reduce profit.

With a thousand in cash in my pocket and my hotbox, I stopped off at a Cuban meat market, made my initial purchase of coke, and went back to my hotel room to test it out. If it measured high, I would make a larger purchase, mix it, and resell it to my friend Carlos, who was running a distribution center and had many ways to get the drug out to the people of South Miami.

The marijuana was on its way, and I could see the money that was about to be made. I ordered a large amount of food and set about planning a big party. It was while the party was going full force that I noticed Vince, my dad's friend, slip out. He flew up to Michigan to see my dad in prison—or so he said—and it slowly dawned on me that he was planning to throw my plans off. I was never sure if my dad had told him to mess with me or if he did it on his own, but within a week I was out hunting him. If I had ever found him, I do believe he would have been dead.

My big drug deal fell apart, and it was probably a good thing, as I learned later that the Feds had been watching me. After the aborted deal, I stayed in front of the supermarket for two days without eating or drinking anything. I had a suitcase under my feet, knives in my boots, the hotbox in the suitcase, and I just didn't know what to do.

The next day, one of my dad's ex-girlfriends had a guy come get me and take me back to where my mom was living. My mom had no clue that I was even in Miami, as she had divorced my dad and was living as far from him as she could.

I stayed with my mom at her trailer for a while, and life became all about how much vodka I could consume. I started each day with a giant cup and sip it away until all my pain and agony of spirit seemed to be drowned. Life no longer made any sense to me, and as I reflected upon my short existence, it already registered as tragic. No matter how hard I looked, I just couldn't see any hope or any way out.

The only path I could see clearly was that of self-destruction. On top of the drinking and whatever drugs I could find, I would go around in a depressed haze and do stupid things just to assure myself that I was still alive. My self-destructive path was rapidly gaining speed and as I limped through the summer, it was becoming apparent that if I didn't make a change for the better, I would probably end up dead. I had reached the point where I just did not care about anything. There were times when I would walk up to a drunk guy who was brandishing a gun and tell him to either shoot me or give me the gun. I would break into various vehicles at the large condos being built and would steal anything I could—simply because I could. I was bored on the outside and hateful on the inside. I made deals with the devil, telling him repeatedly that I would do anything for him if he would just take away the pain.

I ached for money, fame, wealth, and power, but God, in His wisdom, blocked those requests. Even though I felt far from Him, He was never far from me.

11: Drifting In and Out

I survived living with my mom for several months before my younger brother and I decided to go back to Michigan to be closer to Dad. We planned to stay with Granny. Family members told us that they were enrolling us in the Seventh-day Adventist boarding academy in Holly, Michigan, because they were worried that Granny couldn't take care of all of us. We flew to Detroit and hung out at Granny's house until school started, and then we were driven up to Holly to start school.

I was used to living fairly freely, but the school had a rule for everything. I had to be in my room by a certain time, lights had to be turned off at a certain time, I could walk only on the sidewalk for boys, I could not hold the hand of any girl, and I was not allowed to listen to music because they thought I might be tempted to listen to that satanic rock music. Since I was at a low point, I was open to the idea that things might turn around for me. So I decided to try this religion thing—at least for a few weeks.

I was required to attend church once a week and chapel meetings daily. My roommate Rick and I were about as far from God as one could be, so we would sit on the front row and tease the speaker. One time, the speaker got so frustrated that after his talk, he chewed us out for disrespecting him. It was not just him we disrespected but everyone.

My cousin would smuggle in McDonald's Big Macs, which were contraband on that vegetarian campus, and on most weekends I could be found drinking orange vodka on the gymnasium steps while unsuspecting faculty walked all around. I tried my best to fit in, but I saw too much hypocrisy from my point of view, and decided that I had to get out of there.

The epitome of my time at the boarding school—which was a mere two months—happened on the football field. I was a senior at that time, and the boys were told to select a flag football team, which would then play the faculty in an all-star game. I was a very good athlete and was chosen as the captain, so I got to pick the team. We went out intent on destroying the faculty—and were winning. Then, the religion teacher and school chaplain illegally clotheslined my friend Michael running down the sidelines. Michael went down, bounced up like a rocket, and was about to tear the faculty member's head off. I intervened, only to have it happen to me a few plays later. I looked at that chaplain guy and thought, *If this is how Christians behave, then I don't want anything to do with them.*

After two months of trying to fit in, my roommate and I packed up our duffel bags, climbed the back fence of the school, and hiked into the downtown area of Holly, Michigan. Two girls at a pizza restaurant gave us a ride to Pontiac, about forty-five minutes away, and from there we hitchhiked to Canada. The capstone of our trip was getting arrested for wading up to the edge of Niagara Falls—not the brightest thing to do.

Rick and I survived for a couple of weeks on a loaf of bread and a package of bologna. We drank as much coffee as we could because we got free refills and would add as much sugar as we could for nutrition. We also bummed cigarettes and did our best to smoke to keep warm. We made the trip from Canada to Miami in the back of a pickup truck. Rain or shine, we were back there trying not to get blown out, which proved to be quite the experience on the wavy mountain roads of West Virginia and through the downpours of the Carolinas.

We arrived in Miami without any of my relatives knowing where I was, sleeping among some trees on a golf course the first night. We ended up living at my mom's trailer with my youngest brother, Jason. Rick and I both got jobs at a landscaping company, and we did what we could to survive. Rick managed to hang out in Florida for a month and then took a bus back to Michigan. That was the last I ever heard from him.

I tried my best to adjust to life back in Miami, but it was difficult and I quickly got back on the track toward self-destruction. I slipped back into my pitiful pattern of getting drunk in the morning and sleeping my time away. I would get up and lift some weights and drink some more. Life seemed rather hopeless, and in the midst of my despair, my father called from prison with a business opportunity.

He had a grand plan that involved kidnapping my baby brother and taking him into hiding. Since I didn't have anything else going on at the time, I agreed. A woman named Joette showed up in a nice, white Mercedes and whisked me away to the airport. We flew off to North Carolina, where we lived a life of luxury for about three weeks. We stayed in a beautiful mansion that peered out over the valley through a magnificent glass front. A guy named Paul owned the house, and he was hosting several guests for a wild New Year's Eve party. This was the first and last time that I drank something I could not identify, and the first and last time I got sick from drinking too much. It was not a great experience leaning on the bathroom sink trying to vomit—and being so sick that I was unable to.

Big Mike, the jeweler, came to North Carolina from Florida to help out, and all he seemed to do was walk around the estate with a huge marijuana joint in his mouth. It was the largest joint I had ever seen, and every time he passed by, he would offer me a hit. Paul's wife kept telling me stories of Elvis, as she had grown up with "the King," and I found myself wanting to stay and hang out there forever.

I had my run of the place and quickly fit in. Paul arranged for me to have spending money, and so I would buy stuff, party, hang out, go for walks in the hills, and breathe in the crisp air. My little brother Jason was having fun, as well. He had been living in a stuffy little trailer in Miami, and now he had hills to run and places to explore. We could have lived there forever, but as they say, all good things must come to an end.

Our time was cut short because Dad had been thrown into solitary confinement. It had been alleged that he had something to do with Jason's kidnapping. Dad instructed me to fly back to Miami and drop Jason off, then fly to Michigan and hide out while the police continued looking for me. It turned out to be one of the hardest things I ever did—taking my little brother back to Miami and leaving him there alone. I felt as if I was his dad and was shirking my duty to protect him. But I didn't have a choice.

When I got back to Michigan, I went into hiding at my aunt Wanda's house in Clarkston, Michigan, fearing that I would be discovered and charged with being a kidnapper. I didn't know what was really going on, and all I could do was lay low. No one could know where I was, and I couldn't talk to the little brother I desperately missed. It didn't take long for the charges to be dropped, and life returned to normal.

I ended up living at Granny's once again, this time with my two brothers who had gone off the religious deep end. They were attending these Revelation Seminar meetings at the local Adventist church, and I just knew that they had gone crazy. I teased them relentlessly and tried to discourage them from being "religious." I went to church because that was the deal for staying at Granny's, but I tried my best to not learn anything. My favorite position was outside of the morning worship service near the bathroom. Somehow I felt the need to roam the hallway, step outside for a moment—anything but sit in the chairs in the sanctuary.

Meanwhile, my inner rage was still growing. You would think that at some point it would top off, but my reservoir of anger was apparently quite expansive. It was like a cancer inside of me that created a foggy filter through which I viewed the world. I was angry at the hand that life had dealt me, and I didn't trust people one iota.

I graduated from Pontiac Northern Senior High School about the time my dad was released from prison. Through some creative financial meanderings, my father bought a nice house in Waterford, Michigan, and we settled in for a respectable summer. At least that was my hope.

The respectable summer quickly turned into a nightmare. My

mother came to live with us, even though she and Dad had divorced years earlier, and they fought like cats and dogs. I ended up working for a guy who ran a chop shop (he stole and illegally sold car parts), and then decided to enlist in the army just to get away from my parents.

I slipped out and spent the night at a military recruiter's house in Detroit. He partied with me, and when I got drunk, he dropped me off at the facility where I would enlist. The next day, I woke up with a headache and went through all the drills of signing up. I got a job as an MP in West Germany guarding missiles. As I was about to sign my life away and leave for boot camp that day, I panicked and asked them if I could have one more breath of freedom. They agreed, and I walked outside—and then ran and ran and ran. My military career lasted all of one day.

I went back to live with my dad and signed up for college. My plan was to study business at the University of Detroit. Law school was my goal, where I knew I could make a lot of money legitimately working for some not-so-legitimate people.

During the summer, I drank and did whatever I could to pass the time, but inside my life was rotting away under a relentless sun of bitterness. The ugliness of my first eighteen years was starting to permanently alter me, and I felt that I was about to cross a line forever—the line of irreversible damnation. I could feel within me a powerful desire to just walk away from hope and anything good. The worst part was that I did not even care.

The lowlight of that summer was an event that scared me more than I had ever been scared before. Looking back, I can see that God was trying to get my attention yet again. It all started when my cousin and I met these two girls and excitedly planned to take them to a rock concert a few days later.

The only drag was that we knew alcohol would not be allowed, and so we spent a couple of days trying to figure out a way around this obstacle. We bought a plastic ice chest, two six-packs of soda, some chewing gum, and a few corks, and then brought all of that stuff to my cousin's garage. We punched a small hole in the bottom of each can of one six-pack and left the other six-pack alone. Then we filled the emptied cans with whiskey. We stuck a cork in each can of the altered six-pack and sealed them with chewed gum. Placing the corked cans on the bottom of the cooler with ice around them, we set the normal six-pack on top and went off to the concert.

When we got to the amphitheater, the people checking the beverages reached into our cooler and pulled out the top six-pack. Thinking that the other six-pack was also soda, they didn't bother to pull it out. We were in with our valuable contraband. I am pretty sure the people around us wondered how we got blitzed from drinking soda. It didn't take long for us to get inebriated, and I can remember lying on the grass trying to grab the laser lights as they shot up overhead during the concert. The music was loud, the effects were great, and I was just chilling while trying to forget my woes.

After the concert, I was chosen to drive my cousin's big four-wheel drive truck home because I was the most "sober" of the bunch. In actuality, I was the one still able to move my hand to such a degree that I could put the key into the ignition. We all piled into the truck, and with great concentration, I somehow got us in line to leave the parking lot.

It was this big snakelike line, and everyone was in a hurry to drive out the one exit. Everyone was doing their best to weasel in front of us, and my aggravation level was rising with every passing moment. We were only a few cars away from the first significant turn toward the exit when the little car in front of us started to play around. While most people were impatiently trying to go forward, the two young women in this little two-seater took an entirely different tactic to pass the time. Putting their car into reverse, they moved backward until they tapped our front bumper, then moved forward, looking back at us and giggling.

I was about to cuss them out when I noticed that they were flirting with us. Instead of taking it as a compliment, it made me flat out mad. The women in that stupid little car were not giving up, and the white reverse lights lit up again and again. I decided it was time to surprise them.

I reached down, put the truck into low four-wheel drive, and determined to simply run over them. I can still feel the adrenaline rush as I prepared myself for some monster truck action. Just then the guy directing traffic waved us on. I hit the gas with determination because I wanted to hit that little car, but the car shot forward and left us in the dust. With a good head of steam and no little car to run over, the truck lunged forward toward a woman who had opened her door and was getting out of her car. I just knew I was going to run her over.

The scene is still burned into my mind. I threw up my hands and screamed, too drunk to take my foot off the accelerator, as the truck hurdled toward that poor woman. Just before impact, the truck turned left and stopped. I was suddenly very sober, with my eyes and my hands still glued to the steering wheel. I knew that an angel had just reached down from heaven and saved me from a charge of murder.

About three weeks later, I received a call from an admissions representative at Andrews University, asking me if I wanted to enroll. I responded that there was no way I could afford to do so. But Andrews didn't give up on me, and within a week I was on my way there to begin studying pre-law. I didn't mention to anyone that I had a job waiting for me working for a lawyer for the Sicilian mob with a starting salary of one million dollars. He told me that I had been offered the job because of my dad and because I knew how to keep my mouth shut. It seemed like a good deal, so I ran off from my family, thinking I was running away from God, as well.

Boy, was I wrong.

12: Running From God

It is ridiculous to imagine that one could run from God, but I was doing everything I could to do so. I had given up on the idea of running drugs myself, but what could happen if I only defended drug dealers as their lawyer? It would be the best of both worlds! All I really needed was a college degree and a quick trip to law school.

I made the four-hour drive to Andrews University with my dad and uncle. I didn't know anyone at the school and would have gone without much had it not been for my aunt Wanda, who bought me some clean jeans, underwear, and other necessities.

Arriving on campus in the fall of 1983, I was assigned a roommate from central Ohio by the name of Don. Don was an accountant-type of a guy, and he became a good friend by the time our four years were over.

During freshman orientation, I met a guy from Oregon named Jamie. Jamie was an older student who was on fire for God. I learned that his father had ties to the mob on the West Coast. I secretly wondered if he was there to spy on me, and I found out later that he was wondering the same thing about me. But we became friends and spent a lot of time together. We talked about life in the mob, about our dads, and about how God had kept us alive in spite of ourselves. I didn't mind talking about life in the mob or even about my dad, but I soon discovered I was extremely uncomfortable talking about God.

Deep down, I knew that God had supernaturally protected me, but I really wanted to forget about all of that. I had no trouble believing in the supernatural because when I was eight, I remember seeing an evil face appear in the sky. I knew that evil existed, but I truly hoped that if I left evil alone, it would leave me alone. Soon I discovered that it was God and Jamie who wouldn't leave me alone. Jamie kept reminding me of the times I should have crashed, of the times I was shot at and lived, and how God had repeatedly put His hand upon me to spare my life. I did not want to hear it, but as he talked, I grew convicted and started to see that God had "tricked" me into coming to a Christian university.

The night before we were to register for school, Jamie and I stayed up late while he lectured me, hammering me with reminders of God's providence in my life. Over and over he told me that the only reason I was alive was that God had called me into the gospel ministry. I could feel myself being drawn to that choice.

But then I remembered conversations my family had had about how bad ministers were. My family was the type of people who would set the alarms on their watches to ring with some loud, annoying song at noon, just so the minister would know it was time to wrap up his sermon. My family wore ties with pictures of naked ladies on the back and then flipped them up at opportune moments to distract the minister. My family really didn't care about God, to them church was just a social hangout and the minister wasn't seen as a holy man. At one point, my cousin tried to get me to plant some cocaine behind our minister's license plate so we could turn him in to the police. No, I never wanted to be a minister.

Jamie caused my "worst nightmare" to come true, and I found myself signing up as a reluctant religion major. I guess I should not have been surprised, because I clearly remembered that day back in tenth grade when I was walking toward the football field. As I neared the fence surrounding the field, I heard someone say, "You are going to be a minister." It was loud and clear and there was no mistaking it. I even called the local church and told them about the experience, but I am sure they thought I was out of my mind.

The day of registration, I declared my major as pre-seminary, which meant my entire goal was to get into the seminary, where I would be trained to be a minister. You might think I was excited about living the life God had called me to, but in fact, I was miserable. I knew how rotten a person I really was, and somehow I got the idea into my head that I was going to have to do penance to get right with God, even if I didn't love Him. I was willing to work for Him, but I didn't have to like it. I just needed some rules to live by, and so I set about trying to figure out the rules.

I believed that I had to prevent myself from sinning or God would hurl a lightning bolt from heaven to get my attention. I was terrified of sin. I remember sitting on a bench in the middle of a shopping mall determined not to sin. I stared at the floor because I knew that if I looked up and saw a girl and had any evil thought in my mind, it would be a sin and God would "get me."

One night I was walking to the dorm after a late night out, and right in front of the dorm, I stopped. Rain pelted me from a night sky framed by distant lightning. I started yelling at God to leave me alone. I was mad at Him for calling me to be a minister, for the unfair demands that He had placed upon my life. I wanted freedom from Him; I wanted to live life on my own terms. But I was deeply terrified to attempt to do so.

I fought hard and consistently with God. Every quarter I changed my major to something else—architecture, business, physical education. But I kept returning to my religion major because I was deathly afraid that God would condemn me if I didn't. I could handle the condemnation, but not what I thought came with it—an all-out attack from the Almighty. I believed God was ruthless, and the thought that He might love me never even entered my mind.

After my first quarter at Andrews University, I went home not knowing if I would ever return. I had barely survived, passing my classes with a low C average, and my attempt at following the rules was not going well. The day I left for home, the pastor of the university church, Pastor Dwight Nelson, called me because he said God had put me on his heart. He encouraged me and told me that he was excited about what God was going to do in my life in the new year. I hung up on him and cussed out God quietly—"leave me alone."

Back home on break, I needed to make some cash, so I started hanging out with my cousin who was busy restoring a Corvette. He said I could help him for some spending money. I spent a lot of time working on that car and tried to get high off the paint fumes. As I did, the battle within me became overwhelming. I could feel Satan trying to push me away from anything righteous, and my mind was like a motion picture of the past, complete with scenes that I never wanted to remember. The enemy was trying to get me to believe that I was worthless, that I had no hope, and that I was beyond the help of God. It took only about a week for me to cave in under the pressure, and late one night, I opened up the bottom drawer of my cousin's tool chest and lifted out the "sacred" and familiar Jack Daniel's bottle of whiskey. I decided to skip going back to school.

When the Christmas break was nearing its end, I informed my family that I was just going to stay home. My aunt, who I feared more than my dad, got in my face and told me that I was going back to school. For some reason, she planted a fear deep within my bones and I started to reconsider.

God can be fairly sneaky, and one day I got a phone call from a guy my dad knew. This guy had been sentenced to life in prison for murder with an ax, but for some providential reason, had been paroled. As we talked, every other word was Jesus, and this guy really made it clear that without Jesus, there was no hope. Because of the fear I got from my aunt and the Jesus I got from my dad's friend, I made the trek back to Andrews University for yet another quarter of school.

Finishing that year was quite difficult. I had to fight for sanity, for the desire to attend church, and to stay sober. I continued to change my major away from pre-seminary and felt haunted by a God I didn't want to serve but was afraid not to serve.

As the school year came to a close, I was forced to consider what I was going to do for the summer. The previous summer, I had worked with stolen cars, but I wanted to try something different. Because I was now a religion guy who was officially signed up to be a minister, I was encouraged to try selling religious books door to door. It seemed as though anyone who desired to be a minister for my denomination was encouraged—almost expected—to be a "literature evangelist." If I was going to be a minister, I might as well do my time selling books.

After looking around, I settled on a summer job selling religious books in Detroit. My uncle loaned me a car, a 1972 pea-green Pontiac Catalina with no air conditioning, and I worked trying to sell books in the worst part of the inner city.

My job entailed carrying this large leather-looking book bag from door to door and trying to get people to let me into their homes. Once inside, I would set up my little backdrop, which folded into my case, and then I would spin my tale of how these books would transform their lives. I was a terrible salesman, as I wanted to give away the books more than sell them.

I didn't manage to sell much that summer but did develop considerable empathy for all postal employees, as I had some pretty good encounters with mad dogs chasing me. It was a good way to stay in shape, as at least once a week I was forced to run as fast as I could from some unwelcoming dog. My worst encounter involved me jumping onto the roof of my car with the briefcase in front of me as a snarling canine tried to eat me alive.

Working as a literature evangelist didn't really help my faith much. I am not sure if it was because I really didn't want to do it, or if it had more to do with living with my dad and brothers at the time. My dad was out on parole, and we were all living in a nice house. We "played" house together and tried to look like a presentable lot, but it was tough.

My dad would always start off nice when he got out of prison or jail. He would embrace jailhouse religion when he was inside, and that determination to serve God would last about six months. Then he would morph back into some evil dude.

My first time back home after college was right at the time he was starting to revert. I walked into the living room and found my dad sitting on the floor by a chair. He was distraught and was spinning his Beretta around and around. I immediately knew I should back away, but before I could, he locked eyes with me and told me to come in and sit down. I didn't think I had much of a choice, so I went in and sat down on the chair. He proceeded to pour out through drunken tears how disappointed he was in me and how he felt as though I judged him for living life the way he had lived it.

He kept pointing the gun at me, and I began to think that I was really going to die. I became paralyzed with fear, and all emotion evaporated from my body. The longer he talked and the more he spun the gun and pointed it at me, the more completely I just checked out. The spell that he wove that day was broken when the pistol went off as he pointed it directly at me. Shot after shot rang out, and miraculously, not one hit me. When the gun was empty, my dad looked at me and simply said, "I guess you are going to call the cops now." He then got up and walked away and I collapsed on the floor, terrified.

There was no way I was going to call the cops, as I knew my dad would kill me if I did that. I knew that my dad could reach me even from prison, and I was not about to get on his bad side—at least any more than I already was. As the summer continued, I found myself looking forward to going back to school—not because I wanted to learn, but to escape from my insane father, who was growing more evil by the moment.

As I finished up my last month of summer work, I discovered something about our home. It was haunted. There were creepy things happening. Shadows would move around, an ice-cold presence would emerge, my brother would see things, and we could just feel evil. It was terrifying, and I wanted out of there. When I did escape from that house, I never went back. My dad eventually moved, but figuring that maybe *he* was haunted more than that house, I never visited him for more than a day or two. My trust for him had evaporated, and I considered being around him to be courting death and evil.

I returned to Andrews as a pre-seminary major and became a legalistic jerk. I had been so scared the previous summer that I went about trying to save everyone from the clutches of hell. It didn't matter that I had no relationship with God because I thought people just needed to live as I did and everything would be fine. As I tried to convince people to take my "get out of hell free card," the necessity of a relationship with Jesus Christ never dawned on me.

I became a complete hypocrite. I was full of fire and brimstone toward everyone else—while I was fooling around with my girlfriend. I was such a hypocrite that I talked about how everyone else was a hypocrite. I proclaimed a life of purity and holiness, while I lived a life of sin and debauchery. I had perfected the outward appearance, but inside I was mostly rotten.

I preached righteousness, and since I was a fairly good communicator, I even started preaching at area churches. The problem was that I was preaching on the strength of my own personality. I didn't want anything to do with God, but because I felt He was forcing me to serve Him, I figured I could live however I wanted as long as I served Him as a minister.

13: Fear

My four years of college taught me to play the religion game. I learned to talk like a budding theologian, but my college experience was more in learning how to "trick" God and my denomination into thinking I was religious. I knew *about* God and could even use Greek and some Hebrew to explain Him, but I hated Him. If you had asked me who God was, I would have compared Him to some Greek god who was pleased with torturing people on our planet. To me, God was some sort of mythical Thor-like being who acted more like Loki. Thor lived in the heavens and went around carrying lightning bolts for the purpose of using those bolts to zap those who got out of line.

    I wish I could have seen what I had become—a mess. I was full of anger, resentment, hurt, disappointment, and the list went on and on. While things were going great on the outside, I was empty on the inside. I trusted no one and really thought that everyone had it out for me. I had fully convinced myself that the only person I could trust was *me*.

It didn't help that I began a relationship with a girl whose father worked as a high-level executive in my denomination. He was a wonderful man who desired to be the father I had never known. He took me under his wing, bought clothes for me, and taught me how to act. I lost my identity and started taking on his.

However, he also began to teach me about all that was wrong with my denomination. He would tell me when some great leader had a cardinal fall and how the denomination covered it up. He shared with me all of the negative, and I started seeing the denomination as a negative thing, as well.

Eventually, I gritted my teeth enough that I was able to finish my four-year degree in religion and had several job offers ranging from Maryland to Michigan. The Religion Department chair told me he was surprised at all the calls that I received. (I think he saw right through me.) However, I did graduate and I did start my ministerial career in Detroit, Michigan, as an associate minister.

The job started off inauspiciously. When I called the senior pastor to tell him I was ready to start, he was surprised to hear from me! Apparently, no one had informed him that I was coming and he didn't know what to think. I thought he was joking, but when we met for lunch later on in the week, he made it clear to me that he was not joking. He had no idea I was coming, didn't want or need an associate, and told me in no uncertain terms that I was not called into the ministry. Our relationship spiraled downward from then on. I was the young whippersnapper who was supposedly after his job, and he was the old salesman who had gotten into ministry through the back door with no education.

My personal life was no better! I was alone in my apartment and was the assistant minister of two churches working for a pastor who didn't much care for me. I felt as though I couldn't trust a soul—especially God. It felt as if God had cursed me, and I pictured Him up in heaven pulling the strings of my puppet life and laughing. The years of doubt, low self-esteem, abuse, and everything else had done a number on me. Even now, looking back on the first twenty-three years of my life, I wonder how one could go through so much and still be alive. It probably would have been merciful for God to just let me die, but for some reason, He kept me alive. Every part of my heart had been infiltrated with evil and disappointment, and I was numb and in a fog.

On the outside, I was a pastor who lived an apparently awesome life, complete with wingtips and a nice suit, but on the inside, I found myself identifying with psychopaths because I really didn't care about people. There was a deadness to my inner spirit.

I sought reprieve from the deadness inside through pornography. I hated the church, hated being a minister, feared God, but was cocky. I thought I was God's gift to the church because I was a "great" speaker, and people would confirm this regularly. The heart of my work-of-art sermons was only my delivery style. I started speaking at camp meetings and large rallies, and I began to feel that I was moving on up to bigger and better things. I sensed that I could probably make it as a president in the denomination, and I was greedy for more. I was after the position because in my mind, the position meant I was accepted by God.

As I continued earning my way to God, people around me sensed something wasn't right. When the minister I was working with went to the conference president responsible for my churches, I was informed that they didn't think I was called to ministry. "How could they think that?" I fumed. I told my dad about it, and he offered to kill the man—and he was serious. But I just couldn't rationalize being a minister and a murderer at the same time.

My ministerial veneer lasted less than a year and I quit. I moved to Lansing to attend law school and spiraled into self-destruction. When I graduated college, I was full of promise, a budding star in the denomination. A year later, I was in law school trying to run from God as fast as I could. However, God would not leave me alone.

In law school, my fellow students and I would all head off to the local bar each Friday after school to let off steam. I would watch respectful lawyers and judges became idiots under the influence, and it seemed as though everyone around me was getting blitzed, cheating on their wives, or actually having sex in the back of the bar. I could feel God telling me to get out, but I didn't know what else to do.

My confusion lasted for two semesters, and then out of frustration, I left school and went back to Andrews University. Of all places, I enrolled again in the seminary and once again began studying to be a minister. I was a glutton for punishment with no backbone. I didn't want to be a minister, but I now felt as though I didn't have a choice. My destiny was set and the "evil emperor"—God—was forcing me to do His will.

I had no devotional life, only picked up my Bible when I had to for school, and was living a life of debauchery whenever I could. I got drunk repeatedly and lost my soul a little more each time. But in my mind, I was obeying God. He may have forced me into school, but He was not going to change me. I figured I would do His thing for Him and then live any way I wanted for me. It was my compromise, and He would just have to live with it.

However, God didn't "play fair." By the fall, I was content in my hypocrisy and was also involved in the intramural flag football program at the college. I was playing on a team of people I knew, I was still in pretty good shape, and I was especially fast! In one of our first games, my team put me on the line to rush the quarterback because of my speed. Curt was the other defensive end on our team, and he was also fast. When the ball was snapped, both Curt and I sprinted toward the quarterback. The quarterback stepped forward, and Curt and I collided at full speed. The top of his head hit my right orbit, and we both collapsed as if we had been shot.

Dizzy and groggy, the thought of a possible concussion entered my mind. But assuring myself that I was all right, I stayed and watched part of the game before heading back to my apartment. I remember sitting on the couch when a friend came over looking concerned. I said I was all right and refused his offer to take me to the hospital. But when he asked me to put one hand on one side of my face and the other on the other side, I realized that the right side of my face was pushed in about an inch! It took all my strength not to panic, and I agreed to head to the hospital. The next morning, I was scheduled for surgery to rebuild my crushed right orbit.

I was not a happy camper and "knew" that this was God's revenge. I had dared to stand up to Him, and this was how He was getting me back. My hatred of Him boiled hotter than ever. Stuck in that hospital bed all night long, I directed my anger toward God. Hour after hour, I battled with Him, clinging to my stubbornness until I was startled by an early morning visitor.

The anesthesiologist came by with some papers for me to sign releasing the hospital from all liability if I died. It was then that I realized the seriousness of my situation. Yes, I was mad at God, but I had been taught about hell for those who were not righteous, and I could see myself heading straight there! I was terrified and stuck. As I read over the papers and signed my name, I was never so afraid. I did not want to die. Hell was certainly not an enjoyable thought, but neither was being a Christian living for a God I could not trust and who seemed intent on destroying me by allowing all the things He had allowed in my life.

Before I was taken into surgery, the chaplain of the hospital came to pray with me, but I didn't want him to say a word. I did not comprehend the idea that God cared for me or that He would make anything easier on me. I just wanted Him to leave me alone—but keep me out of hell. After the surgery, my right eyelid did not seal correctly, causing my eye to tear up at the strangest times, which kept me from seeing out of that eye.

I tried working at various jobs, but ended up unemployed, living in a small basement apartment, and drinking alcohol. Life became all about escaping creditors and watching late-night TV. Yet I thought I was beating God at His own game. I had somehow found a way to dodge His cruel demand of me, and so I just wasted my life and laughed in His face. Yet I was miserable.

Years ago, I had heard Chuck Swindoll say, "God takes impossible people, breaks them down until they cannot go any further, and then calls them to a task that only they can do." I was finally near that point and tried to call out to God, but I was afraid that I was too far gone. Beyond hopeless, I was pretty sure I had committed the unforgiveable sin, but I hated where I was, so I was desperate to try anything—including God.

It is because of that experience that I am writing this book. I understand how one can feel, how desperate one can get, how far one can fall. Evil has a way of distorting all things, and yet, even in such times, God can still do miracles. He did many in my life, and more important, He can still do one in your life, as well!

14: Pleasing God . . . Earning Love?

When I got out of the hospital, I looked like I had been in a bad fight. The entire right side of my face was swollen, and my orbit had that wonderful yellow-and-black shade to it. I did not feel so good—on the outside or the inside. I felt overwhelmed by my past and could not see any hope for my future. I knew that I had been called to be a pastor, but that seemed unlikely now, and so I was faced with a grim future while holding a worthless degree in religion.

I thought about going back to law school, about getting a doctoral degree in psychology, about just ending my life. Have you ever felt so bleak, so hopeless, that you felt as though you were in a suffocating tunnel that kept getting smaller and smaller and there was no pinhole of hope? Someone once termed the phrase, "The dark night of the soul," and I knew that I was in the midst of such darkness. I thrashed around in darkness while hearing the tempter's voice: "You can make money. You were never supposed to be a minister. There is no hope for you. Your only future is in a life of crime." I could feel Satan wanting to suck me down into the mire of evil, and yet God persisted in His pursuit of me. I felt that He should have let me go because there was nothing good within me. I am not sure if it was because Granny was praying or if God was just determined, but in the midst of the dark, a slight glimmer emerged, and I felt a force within me directing me to go back to school and get back into ministry.

The idea of me being a minister seemed asinine to me, yet it seemed to be the way out. I enrolled in the Andrews University Graduate School, this time pursuing a dual degree in psychology and religion. I thought this combination would be helpful to me and also get me back into the religious line of thinking. I rented an apartment on campus and started to pour everything I had into God. I did not feel anything different, but I thought I would find Him somewhere.

I started attending church, reading my Bible, and attempting to pray. In retrospect, what I was doing was trying to "earn" a relationship with God and once again "look the part." Using my poor relationship with my dad as a template, I was off to force God to "fit" as my father. I knew it took living a certain way to please my earthly father, so I figured that living a godly life—even though I was faking it—would please God.

I was on my way to sainthood and was feeling pretty good. My works were becoming what I thought they should be, and I was starting to feel that I was actually saved—good enough to get into heaven. But below the surface of my existence, deep within my soul, my rebellious nature and inner anger were still brewing, and I was doing my best to hold them in check.

Sigmund Freud said that a person is like a house, with an attic, main level, and basement. The attic is the best part of the mind. It is where all the good thoughts and desires are kept. The basement is full of spider webs and bad thoughts, and the main part of the house is what people see, the balance between the attic and the basement.

All of my past was in the basement of my mind, and so I did what any red-blooded male would do—I bolted the door and tried like crazy to keep all the evil from leaking out. All the garbage from my past, all the abuse, all the uncertainty, my temper and anger—you name it, I cracked open the basement door, and tossed it all in so it wouldn't escape.

During this time, I met a young woman who made the mistake of smiling at me. I was walking through the architecture building at Andrews University, studying my Hebrew vocabulary cards, when this beautiful young lady just happened to look up from her design desk as I ambled by. I smiled back and kept on walking. However, I tried to memorize her face so I could look her up in the *Cast,* a picture directory of everyone at Andrews University.

I pondered what romantic thing I would do and settled on sending her a note accompanied by a rose. After sending the rose and not getting any response, I was puzzled. So I walked through the architecture building again. I didn't see her, but there was a drawing on her desk with her name on it. It was then that I realized I had sent the rose to the wrong person!

Determining to be a bit more careful this time, I went out and bought a bud vase with a rose and put a card on her desk inviting her out on a blind date to an Italian restaurant. I made sure no one saw me put it on her desk and ran home as fast as I could to wait for her call. (This was before the cell phone era.)

And she did call! Twenty-five years later, I am sure she wonders what she got herself into, but at the time, I did my best to get to know her. I told her about my past on our first date and then dropped her off at her dorm. November passed, and I didn't hear from her. December came and went, and still nothing. (I sent her a Christmas card just to be nice.) January rolled around, along with the new quarter, and still I had not heard a word from Toria.

Then the phone rang. Somehow, during the holiday break, she had come to her senses and decided to get to know me. (Either that or she drank some spiced eggnog.) For the next three weeks, we were inseparable. We played racquetball, talked, laughed, joked, studied, and just did that dating thing. I had a drafting table installed in my apartment so she could use it whenever she wanted. Things were progressing well, and after dating a grand total of three weeks, it was arranged that I would drive down with her to Kentucky to visit her parents.

Upon my arrival in Kentucky, the first thing her dad did was challenge me to a game of arm wrestling. I thought he was joking, but he was serious. Thankfully, I beat him, but it really didn't bode well.

I don't think I made a good impression on either her father or her mother. Looking back on it, they may have seen some of the stuff poking out from under the basement door.

I survived that weekend, but the next weekend proved to be even more eventful. One night early that week, I got the strange idea that I should ask Toria to marry me. Why not? So, the next day, we talked about it and decided that we would fly to Las Vegas and get hitched. I know what you are thinking. *How could they do something so rash?* Well, my basement door was shut and I looked as if I had everything together, and this incredible woman saw me as this adventuresome guy who loved God. It was the perfect . . . façade!

Just minutes after the wheels of the plane lifted from the Chicago runway, we began to doubt that we were really going to tie the knot. But after officially dating for three weeks, we were joined in holy matrimony. If you had asked me if I knew what I was doing, I would have said, "Certainly." After all, she was certainly mature at the ripe old age of nineteen, and I was certainly mature at the even riper age of twenty-three. I didn't make much of the fact that this was the only thing I had ever done that surprised my father.

We eloped at the Candlelight Wedding Chapel, right across the street from a casino. As we were driving around on our honeymoon, we determined to have the "perfect" relationship. We knew that many relationships did not work out, so we wanted to be the ones who would help all those other folk who were going to experience difficulties. We just knew our relationship would be godly, and we wanted it built on communication. We started reading every book we could get our hands on that had anything to do with marriage because our goal was to write the perfect marriage book. We were going to call it "Crazy Glue," as it was to be a book about how to put together a wonderful marriage with God as the "glue."

I am sure those around us thought that we had gone crazy. When we returned to Andrews, we were afraid to tell anyone what we had done. My new wife's mom drove all night and showed up early the next morning to talk her daughter out of this strange marriage. But when she knocked on my apartment door, I had to tell her that her daughter was not there. She was confused, so I explained that we had not told anyone what we had done, and that Toria had spent the night in her dorm room. Her mom eventually tracked her down, and though I am not sure what was actually said, she became convinced that this incredible young woman knew what she was doing.

We were sure that we could make it all work and that God had let us choose our destiny, but I now wish that some graceful saint would have stepped in to share some godly counsel. Of course, that was not possible because my lack of trust in people also kept me from accepting that kind of accountability. I suffered from the Lone Ranger complex. I thought I was above all the problems of this world and could solve them simply by my "great" wisdom.

As I consider that time in my life, I am grateful that the Lord extended His hand of grace to me by bringing such a woman into my life. She has never left my side. She has prayed for me, has encouraged me, and has challenged me to be a better husband, father, and man of God. To this day, my wife remains my hero and pillar of strength in my life.

I eventually finished my master's degree, and my bride completed her degree in architecture. As we considered our future, I was toying with going forward to pursue my doctoral degree in counseling psychology. She encouraged me to do what I needed to do, but I was uncertain. This is when a woman I was working for called me into her office.

Herdley worked for a university department that provided academic guidance and testing, and I had been working with her in developing a peer helper network at the school. As a result, we had spent a great deal of time together, and she had gotten to know me fairly well. She graciously waded into my life and asked me a question: "Pat, do you think you have an anger problem?" I could not believe she had asked that question, and my fuse was lit. "Me? An anger problem? How could you think such a thing?"

15: Japan

In the midst of our decision-making process about life after graduation, the Japan Union of our denomination sent a representative to Andrews to gather college-aged folk who were interested in serving in the mission field in Japan. Pastor Kim came to Andrews to do the recruiting. My wife was familiar with Pastor Kim, as she had previously served as a student missionary for a year in Japan.

I went with her to talk with Pastor Kim, and he offered us a two-year stipend volunteer position at the Chiba English Language Institute. We accepted with the understanding that I could establish an English language church for the local Japanese to attend. We would be using the carrot of teaching people English to get them to study the Bible with us. Now, being from Detroit, I had a certain amount of prejudice against Japan as America's direct competition in the automotive industry, and if it weren't for a dream I had about running from God, I don't think I would have actually gone.

We flew off to the Land of the Rising Sun, but as soon as we arrived, it looked more like the sun was constantly setting for us. We had been promised an apartment, but that did not materialize. Instead, we slept at Pastor Kim's house on the floor in a spare room.

My world went from consistency to mayhem. My job was different, my life was different, and if anyone experienced culture shock—it was me. I had no idea what the food before me really was, I couldn't understand the language, and the people were protesting our country's involvement in the Gulf War, which had just begun. There was no Internet or cell phones for us, so I felt like I was drowning in an unfamiliar culture. McDonald's and Dunkin Donuts were my only reminders of the good ol' U.S.A. Even though I scratched and clawed for a thankful spirit, my anger continued to build. I pushed it deeper and deeper inside, and pushed out everything good to make room.

My wife, however, thrived in this environment—it was like a high school reunion for her. She knew many of the people, could understand a great deal of the language, and was enjoying teaching others how to speak English.

By the time we moved into a small apartment, I was teetering on the brink of a nervous breakdown. Every night I would sit up rocking until my stomach stopped churning. Then I got the news that Granny, the rock of my life, had died. I flew back to the States to perform her funeral.

While I was there, I found out that my dad had remarried. Wanting to spend some time with my dad, I jumped at the chance to take him to see his cousin. Unfortunately, the meeting was in a bar in downtown Detroit. I managed to drink nothing more than soft drinks, but I was a nervous mess just being in that environment. My dad sat near my cousin, who was a cop, at one end of a large table filled with fifteen people. I sat at the other end hoping against hope that Dad wouldn't get drunk, become belligerent, and start a brawl.

Just a few minutes after sitting down, a woman with a gaunt face and long, stringy hair walked up and introduced herself as a psychic. I suddenly felt like vomiting, as I knew we were about to have a supernatural encounter of the worst kind.

She began reading palms. Not having anything good to report about my cousin, she moved on to my father. Once again, having only evil things to report, she summed up by warning that death was near. Looking at me, she rasped, "Hey, what about you?" I didn't respond and looked away. Raising her voice, she boldly proclaimed that she wanted to read my palm. I gave her a cold stare that said, "Don't even breathe my way." Not giving up, she came slithering toward me. That's when my inebriated cousin, the Detroit cop, yelled some cusswords at her. To paraphrase, he yelled, "Hey, he works for the other guy!" Startled into silence, she turned and walked away. I was in awe. I couldn't believe that my cousin had defended me—or that he knew the side I represented.

When I got back to Japan, my stress intensified. I was not able to sleep much, and each night found me on the verge of a panic attack. The anger that had been building within me reached its climax, and one night at the English language school, I almost got into a fistfight with Pastor Kim. I ended up storming out of the office with clenched fists. I was unraveling fast. My anger now controlled me, and it had escalated into pure rage. When it rose to the surface, I would explode, destroying anything and anyone in my path.

Determined to get away from the English language school, the church transferred me to the college and I became an official missionary of the denomination. I imagine that they did not know what to do with me, and because I had a rage problem combined with a cockiness problem, they thought shipping me out to the country would do me good.

We moved to the village of Otaki, got a bigger apartment, bought a car, and life was looking up—for a little while. Eventually, even that promotion was not enough, and my rage and rebellion surfaced once again. I can see now that God was taking me on a journey that was removing every possible distraction from my life. We lived in a village in the middle of nowhere with no communication with anyone outside of an occasional letter. I had nothing to fall back on. I couldn't go to the movies, watch TV, listen to anything but the news on Armed Forces Radio, and I couldn't even read the paper. I was left to face myself, which was very discouraging, to say the least.

However, I was a good escape artist, and after spending two years in Japan, I came up with a way out. I decided that we should leave Japan. My wife reluctantly agreed, and we returned to the States as I barely hung on to sanity.

And that is when I completely fell apart.

16: No Trust in Anyone

Returning from the mission field takes some adjustment, and we had no idea where we fit in. In the midst of our pondering about the future, we got some great news. My wonderful wife was pregnant! You would think this would have settled my spirit, as the joy of being a father was a dream that I had always cherished.

My euphoria lasted only a short while, however, because of my mistrust of everyone—including my wife. From early on in my life, I had had people burn me. My wife, the one person who had never done anything wrong to me, was trying to get me to trust her, but I was acting like an irrational idiot toward her. We entered into a rocky time where I went off the deep end and she got down on her knees and interceded for me.

In my attempt to run from life, I was accepted into the doctoral program of the psychology department at Indiana State University. Living in denial and barely able to breathe from the stench of my own problems, I was determined to become a psychologist and help others with theirs. You would think I would have finally surrendered my problems to God, but I just stacked them on the ever-growing "this is God's fault" pile. I now had issues with marriage, children, being the son of a drug dealer, hating my denomination, and the list went on and on and on. I started drinking again to hide the pain and tried to do anything—constructive or destructive—that would deaden the agony. I was miserable, lost a lot of weight, and was losing my mind and soul. It was only the grace of God that kept me alive.

This state of chaos continued for several months until a colleague at ISU invited me to attend church with her at the Maplewood Christian Church. I was shocked that anyone would invite me to church, but I was desperate, and so I went, wary that the antichrist would grab me upon entering. What actually grabbed me was the people's complete acceptance of me just as I was. Their acceptance gave me a wonderful sense of God's presence in my life. I made an appointment to speak to the pastor, and he shared with me the simple message of God's grace, which I had somehow repeatedly missed. I attended Bible studies, morning and evening services, and I tried to learn all I could about God's love. It was a wonderful experience that culminated one Easter morning.

I was driving down Highway 31 in northern Indiana heading back to school when the Lord clearly told me that I needed to choose who I was going to serve. I instantly knew what that meant, and with tears flowing, I agreed to follow Jesus from my heart. I had finally realized that I could no longer do what I was doing without exploding. As I cried, I talked to Jesus, and for the first time in my life, I was open and honest with Him and could hear Him breathe as He wrapped His arms around me.

Three months after that day, a small Christian church in Atwood, Illinois, called me to serve as their pastor, and I became the shepherd of a small flock with limited hope. Their building had burned down, and they had dwindled down to twenty-nine souls trying to figure out if they had any purpose or not. Within one year, an amazing thing occurred. We built a new building, attendance shot up to ninety-nine, and the community was all abuzz.

However, the greatest thing during this time for me was that God healed my relationship with my wife. It was as if He reached down inside my brain and did some rewiring. I could sense a real change taking place within me for the very first time. My wife and I started talking, praying, and encouraging each other (although she had always done this for me), and that little church in Atwood reached out to us as the Holly church had done in my earlier days. We were loved, encouraged, uplifted, and embraced, and our marriage started to grow in an incredible way. A few months later, our second child was conceived, and from all outward appearances, life was grand. I had a new lease on life, a new growing church, a wonderful family, and I was chipping away at my doctoral degree in psychology.

But one major problem remained. I had not allowed God to do any deep work on my soul. I was making outward choices that needed to be made, but inwardly I still had a lot of trust issues with Jesus. Part of that trust issue was that I did not want to totally surrender to God because I really didn't want to limit how I was going to live. I was still holding back and thought that I could serve God and still just be me—well, at least a nicer version of me. I didn't want to be told how I was to live! I did not want to take God that seriously.

A minister friend and I went to see a movie that I do not like to admit that I saw. It was an NC-17 movie called *Showgirls,* and it was pretty much a pornographic movie. I felt as though it wouldn't bother me to see it, and my ministerial colleague also felt it was OK to watch. I was back to the perfect hypocrite. I served God publicly, but inwardly I lived as I wanted. I still would go only so far when it came to God.

However, God didn't give up on me (as usual), and started pestering me through the Holy Spirit. I was aggravated but could sense that God was calling me to take Him seriously. I didn't want to do it but thought that perhaps I should try. Perhaps—*perhaps*—if I really put my all into getting to know Jesus, it would make me a better person.

I remembered back in college that there was this pastor in Kalamazoo who would get up and spend an hour with God every morning. He said it was the key and that we should all do it. I thought he was pretty much off his rocker. Who in their right mind would get up early to read the Bible and pray? As I pondered what the Holy Spirit was telling me, I decided that I would give it a try. How hard could it be?

It was terrible. The first morning, with my cup of hot java in hand,

I closed my eyes and prayed. Then I read a bit from my Bible and glanced at the clock. Only five minutes had passed. I had determined to spend an hour with God and I had not gone past five minutes! Taking a deep breath, I read my Bible for fifty-nine minutes. I had prayed for one minute and had read the Bible for fifty-nine—one hour!

I made some adjustments after that frustrating morning. I got into the routine of writing a letter to God in a prayer journal, jotting down a list of people to pray for, and then read at least five chapters from the Bible, a habit that I still do years later. After about a year, I started looking forward to my hour in the morning, and as I started to learn more about Jesus through this time, a subtle change happened in my life. I began to fall in love with Jesus, and it was that love that finally opened me up enough for the Holy Spirit to slip inside and reveal to me something that scared me straight.

17: Satan Is Real . . . But God Is All-Powerful

In the winter of 1996, I was carrying my four-year-old daughter and walking toward the side door of the Loogootee Christian Church in Indiana, which was next door to the church parsonage where my family and I lived. The door was unlocked, and, peering through the glass, I could see that the lights were on in the sanctuary. Assuming the worship team was preparing for the weekend service, I entered and found a man and a woman seated in the front pew. I politely asked them if I could help them, and they informed me that they were looking for the pastor. I responded that I was the pastor and would be happy to talk to them and would be right back after running my daughter back home.

Depositing my daughter in my wife's arms, I called a friend of mine to come over to the church just in case I needed some help. Returning to my guests, I sat directly across from them in the Communion chairs facing the congregation. They glanced at each other, and the woman whispered, "Should we tell him?" I had no idea what they were about to say, but judging by their appearance, I was preparing for the worst. The man had a sword strapped to his side, they were both wearing all black, both had black hair and white faces, and both were wearing shirts declaring their allegiance to Satan.

The lady turned to me and blurted, "We are witches." Instantly, the hair stood up on the back of my neck, and I desperately wanted to say, "Thanks for coming—see you later." Instead, I silently prayed for wisdom to understand what was going on. I asked them what had brought them to the church, and they told me that they were tired of the voices in their heads and wanted out. They had sensed God's presence while walking by the church and knew they could get help there. When they tried the door, it was unlocked, so they came in. After counseling with them, I baptized the young man on the spot.

My friend Keevin and I went to the man's home, which was decorated with upside-down stolen crosses, and helped him clean up the area and dedicate it to God. He took us into his bedroom where he opened the lid on a cooler, and a white gaslike substance started coming out. It looked like fog. I was officially freaked out and prayed as fast as I could that God would protect us. I picked up the young man's evil robe and spread it out, and we started putting things on it that needed to be discarded. There were books of chants and spells and other evil things, as well.

Keevin and I took the stuff, walked out to my car, and opened up the trunk. Before I put the stuff in there, Keevin and I prayed that God would protect the trunk and us from the evil that we had just experienced. We drove over to the church, got out of the car, and looked at each other, not having any idea what to do with these things. After a brief discussion, we decided to put it in the burn barrel behind the church, near my garage. We stuffed it all inside the burn barrel and poured gasoline on it so it would burn up faster. We wanted to make sure that all of it burned completely.

I lit a match, stood back, and tossed the burning match into the barrel, certain that when the flames got wind of the gas fumes, the contents of the barrel would go *Boom!* The match landed on the stuff, but even though the flame was burning, the contents did not catch fire. I turned to Keevin and we started to pray. We tossed more matches in, and the gasoline-soaked contents very slowly started to burn. A large cloud of smoke began rising from the barrel. When it got about twenty feet in the air, it stopped rising—right before our eyes—as if it hit an invisible ceiling. The smoke began to build up, swirled around a bit, and then came back down and headed for Keevin and me. I was absolutely paralyzed with fear. Keevin reached up, made the sign of the cross in the air, and rebuked the smoke in the name of Jesus. It immediately vanished. Later, after the smoke tried to intimidate us once more, the contents of the barrel finally burned up, and Keevin and I went to our homes in silence.

The experience had lasted all night, and I was terrified. I was realizing just what we were dealing with, and the idea that Satan was alive and well was something that I did not want to face. In my mind, I had hoped that Satan was not real and that evil did not really exist. I was hoping for living a good life and trying to believe that this was all that was really needed.

The next day I tried to forget what had happened, and that worked until the sun went down. When darkness fell, it felt as though an evil presence enveloped the area all around our house. Stepping out of my house to walk to the church, I felt chills all over my body, and I immediately came back in and closed the door. My wife asked me what was wrong, and I told her that I was terrified to go outside. I really felt that something evil was standing between the house and the church door, and I was deathly afraid.

As I sat in my house, afraid to go next door, the name of a man came to my mind. I had heard him speak in Terre Haute, Indiana, years earlier. His name was Ben Alexander, and he was a former spiritualist who had led séances in England years earlier. He had formed a ministry called ESP (Exposing Satan's Power), and I had heard him share the reality of Satan and how evil impacts our world. When I had heard him speak, I thought he was a bit off, but the previous night had brought his stories to my mind.

I found my copy of his book and saw that he lived near Tampa, Florida. Calling information, I got his telephone number and was surprised that he himself answered. I was never so happy to talk with anyone in my life! I quickly recounted my experience and shared with him my intense fear. After listening patiently, he shared with me the reality that God was more powerful than Satan. He reminded me of 2 Timothy 1:7: "For God has not given us a spirit of fear, but of power and of love and of a sound mind," and 1 John 4:4: "He who is in you is greater than he who is in the world." He encouraged me by making it clear that God was in me, that God is more powerful than evil, and that because of that, I had nothing to fear. He told me to claim the power of God and to walk outside and be confident. I thanked him, hung up the phone, and prayed like I had never prayed before.

I walked up to my door, twisted the doorknob, opened the door slowly, and repeated the two verses aloud over and over, my heart pounding with every step. I knew that Satan wanted me to fear him, but in the heat of the battle, I was confident that God was greater. I made it to the church, and in my spirit I knew God was telling me that I was not to be afraid.

I thought my class in spiritual warfare was over, but God was not done working yet. A few years earlier, I had met a Pentecostal pastor at the Promise Keepers Clergy Conference in Atlanta, Georgia. During that conference, we were challenged to find someone from a different belief system and ask him to pray for us. I had always spoken ill of the Pentecostals, so I felt I needed to ask a Pentecostal to pray for me. Not having a clue as to how to find one, I just tapped the shoulder of the guy in front of me and asked, "You wouldn't happen to be a Pentecostal pastor, would you?" Remarkably, he was! I told him that I felt he needed to pray with me, and so he did. We traded business cards and I forgot all about it—until a few years later when he called me out of the blue.

It was after my spiritual warfare experience that he called me up one evening and asked if I remembered him. I told him I vaguely did, and he responded by telling me something that blew me away. He said that while he had been praying, God had told him to invite me to come and preach at his church in northern Ohio.

"Excuse me? God said *what*?" I fumbled. He repeated that he was sure I was to come to his church to preach. I thought he was crazy, but with all that had been happening in my life, I knew I shouldn't rule anything out. I told him I would pray about it, and as I did, I sensed in a deep, inner way that God did indeed wanted me to accept his invitation.

It did not make any sense, but my family and I packed up and made the drive at the end of January, through an ice storm—during the Super Bowl, no less. We showed up in Ohio and he welcomed us into his home. He did not know us from Adam but treated us like long-lost kinfolk. Showing us around his little church, he informed me that they had two services and that I was to preach at both of them and then again on Sunday night.

I had prepared a sermon and knew that I could wing one for Sunday night, so I was not too worried about it. I was a little nervous about being in a Pentecostal church, as I had never set foot in one my entire life. To be honest, I had always thought that the spirit in the Pentecostal church was not from God.

I arrived early at the New Life Church of God to greet everyone as they entered. It was a small building that could probably hold 120 people if everyone packed in tight. The service started, and Dode, the Pentecostal preacher who had invited me to preach, leaned over to me and said, "Just preach whatever God has put on your heart and then ask if anyone wants to be prayed for at the end." It made sense, so when it came time to preach, I got up, walked over to the pulpit, and as I spread out my notes to begin my sermon, it was as if God shut off my brain.

I didn't know what to say, and as I paused and looked out over the people, I felt like it was my first sermon. Then words started coming to my mind and I just started talking. It was the most powerful sermon I had ever preached, and it went on for about two hours. People went home, got other people, and brought them back to the church while I was still speaking. I had never seen anything like it before. Then, when I asked if anyone wanted prayer, the entire church formed a line and approached me one by one. I prayed about each one's request. It was a draining but wonderful time.

As the last person in line walked toward me, she started weeping uncontrollably. She looked to be in her late twenties and was accompanied by an older woman I took to be her mother. The young woman was in obvious misery, and as she got closer, she almost collapsed from the sobs. I had her sit in the front pew and then told her I was going to pray for her.

When I approached her, she started wailing all the more, so I stepped back and asked the older woman, who turned out to be her friend, what had happened to her. She told me that she had been sexually assaulted and was battling to recover from it. I instantly thought I understood. She had come up for prayer, I was a male stranger, and I figured my presence had unsettled her.

I cautiously approached her again and stepped to the side so I wouldn't be directly in front of her and calmly shared with her that I was going to pray for her. She nodded that she understood. I reached out to lay my hand on her head, but right before I touched her, she went berserk. She started slamming her head into the corner of the wooden pew and wouldn't stop. I thought she was going to kill herself, so I instructed the women nearby to lay her on the floor as I thought perhaps she was having a seizure. When they laid her on the floor, she kept lifting up her head, moaning loudly, then slamming her head on the hard wooden floor. I did not know what to do, so I sat down on the floor and cradled her head in my hands to prevent her from hurting herself more. It all happened so fast that I was operating on sheer reflex.

As I sat there trying to decide what to do, she tipped her head back, looked right into my eyes, let out a scream, and then a deep masculine voice came out of her that said, "She's ours." I was in for a battle with a demon. I began praying aloud, deeply and intensely, and all the people in the church were praying also. Eventually, the woman appeared to vomit, but nothing came out. Then she fell asleep and then woke up calm with no idea of what had happened. She got up off the floor and began praising Jesus. Everyone was so excited, and yet I felt like a wet noodle on the floor. My head was spinning from what had just happened.

Two unusual things happened during this time that started a series of events that God used to officially move me from where I was to where I knew I needed to be.

The first involved a woman with gangrene in her leg. She was scheduled to have surgery on her left leg and was facing the possibility of amputation. I was impressed to go to her house and pray with her, and when I did, her leg was healed right before our eyes.

The second event occurred when I was invited to go to a Catholic prayer meeting. Strangely enough, I didn't think Catholics were Christians, either. Each person present was prayed for in this meeting. I had been sitting cross-legged on the floor, but when it was my turn, I laid down while they prayed over me. It was quite soothing, but the prayer leader interrupted the prayer and said, "Something is wrong. I cannot stand before him and pray." She repeated it, then looked directly at me and said that God was protecting me and wanted me to know that He was all I needed.

After two months of these intense, almost crazy experiences, I developed gastritis and was a nervous wreck. The experiences themselves didn't cause the gastritis; it developed because I now knew that God was real, that Satan was real, that spiritual warfare was real, and that God wanted me to get serious about my faith and about serving Him. I knew that this would mean giving up many of my small sins and allowing Him total access to my heart—and that scared me more than anything else. Yet from that time onward, I knew there would never be any turning back because I realized that God was serious, that Satan was serious, and that I needed to get serious, too.

It was in Loogootee that I discovered who Jesus was, and it transformed me. More accurately, it finally set me on the right path so that God could transform me into His character and image as I fell deeper and deeper in love with Him. I finally started to understand what loving God was all about, and the seeds finally started to grow. My faith went from worrying about leaving God, to understanding and knowing that I would never walk away from the living and all-powerful God—even if at times I did not understand Him or struggled with trusting Him.

18: The Seeds of a Motorcycle Outreach

In January of 2000, I accepted a call to become the senior pastor of the Central Christian Church in Snohomish, Washington. We moved from the Midwest and arrived to the beauty of mountains and greenery. We came to serve a church that had been averaging about 166 in worship attendance, and within one year the attendance skyrocketed to 400. In the midst of this incredible growth, I began to reconsider what church was all about.

The church featured a motorcycle ministry called Midnight Cry. It was led by Pastor Dean Ekloff, a former drug and alcohol abuser who had rambled the streets of Snohomish looking for no good. Dean told me that he would walk down the sidewalk in downtown Snohomish and everyone would move to the other side to avoid him. He was certainly trouble, but even he was no match for God's Holy Spirit. The Lord got a hold of him and powerfully transformed him.

Through his ministry, Dean introduced me to unconditional love for all people and to working with the hurting, the burned, the bored, and the bypassed. The church was a very welcoming place—you couldn't get in the door without a bear hug from the greeter. It was also a very real place. People were allowed to be who they were. If you were struggling, someone would come alongside you to support and encourage you. All were allowed to be "in process."

As part of Dean's ministry, he was allowed into biker gangs to conduct weddings and funerals; they loved Dean for his authentic and real faith. However, the people in our community did not know what to think about Dean. Some thought of him and the people in his ministry as uneducated and up to no good, but as I continued getting to know him, I came to deeply respect him for his humble heart.

I took what I had learned from Midnight Cry with me as I served a church in northern California. While there, I dusted off my riding skills and purchased a motorcycle after going a long time without riding. I started off small with a Yamaha 250, then transitioned to a 650, and then an 1100 before finally purchasing a Harley Davidson Softail Custom—my baby.

Soon I moved my family to Florida and to serving a church that was going through a difficult time. God blessed, and the church more than doubled in attendance. We added an additional service, welcomed new members, and were really starting to resemble our multiracial community. But then, a few leaders of the church decided they were uncomfortable with the growth, and I painfully watched as they began bickering. As I struggled to keep people focused on reaching the lost for Christ, it soon became clear to me that most churches have their hands full developing those who already call the church their home. Frustrated with this, I thought about all those in the community who did not know Jesus. What do we do with them? Who will serve as missionaries in our culture to reach those who do not know Him?

As a minister, it was always pressed upon me that I had to be aware of the people I served and that politics are important to keeping everyone happy in a church. A large part of my salary was dependent upon pleasing people, and I soon realized that my calling was not one of politics but of simply reaching out and helping people. I just wanted to be me, and I wanted people to be themselves. I thought of the church as a place for hurting people to grow so that they could become more like Jesus. But it seemed to be a place of façades. We don't tell people what is going on with our lives because we do not want to be judged. We don't tell people we are struggling with this or that because we expect to be dealt with harshly.

I read two books that impacted me greatly at this time.

The first was *Messy Spirituality*, by Michael Yaconelli. He challenged me to not make myself a gatekeeper for who could come to Christ. "Nothing makes people in the church more angry than grace. It's ironic: we stumble into a party we weren't invited to and find the uninvited standing at the door making sure no other uninviteds get in. Then a strange phenomenon occurs: as soon as we are included in the party because of Jesus' irresponsible love, we decide to make grace 'more responsible' by becoming self-appointed Kingdom Monitors, guarding the kingdom of God, keeping the riffraff out (which, as I understand it, are who the kingdom of God is supposed to include)."[1] I did not want to be a "kingdom monitor." I wanted the Holy Spirit to be the Kingdom Monitor, and the only thing I wanted to do was to shout to the people that Jesus loves them. It sounded so wonderful to have a church where people could really understand the love of God. What could be wrong with that?

The second book was *What's So Amazing About Grace?* by Philip Yancey. He shared a story about a friend of his who works with the down-and-out in Chicago:

> A prostitute came to me in wretched straits, homeless, sick, unable to buy food for her two-year-old daughter. Through sobs and tears, she told me she had been renting out her daughter—two years old!—to men interested in kinky sex. She made more renting out her daughter for an hour than she could earn on her own in a night. She had to do it, she said, to support her own drug habit. I could hardly bear hearing her sordid story. For one thing, it made me legally liable—I'm required to report cases of child abuse. I had no idea what to say to this woman.
>
> At last I asked her if she had ever thought of going to a

church for help. I will never forget the look of pure, naïve shock that crossed her face. "Church!" she cried. "Why would I ever go there? I was already feeling terrible about myself. They'd just make me feel worse."[2]

As I struggled with how church should be done, I found myself reading and re-reading the Gospels and the book of Acts so that I could see how Jesus did church. I wanted to be the church that Jesus lived. Was that possible? It was then that God started to weave into my heart a call for a motorcycle outreach to reach out to those who did not know Jesus as their Lord and Savior. When I shared this with a friend of mine, Pee Wee, he resonated with the idea, and SimpleHobo Ministries was born.

SimpleHobo Ministries is an independent Adventist ministry designed to be a chaplain to our community, state, and world. We desire to plant seeds of hope in the hearts of individuals who do not know Jesus, and to encourage those who do. It has been my honor to be a part of SimpleHobo, and I believe God has great things in store for this ministry, including—we hope—the first motorcycle church in the Adventist denomination. I believe that my life story has culminated in making me into the evangelist that God has called me to be. As part of SimpleHobo, I also run a small Christian counseling center called Family4Today, which offers counseling services for those with addictions.

It has been an amazing journey, and I am eternally grateful for my Lord and Savior, Jesus Christ, who saved a wretch like me.

---

1. Michael Yaconelli, *Messy Spirituality* (Grand Rapids, MI: Zondervan, 2002), 47.
2. Philip Yancey, *What's So Amazing About Grace?* (Grand Rapids, MI: Zondervan, 2002), 11.

Epilogue: Where I Am Today

I turned forty-nine this year, and I wish that I could report that my spiritual life has reached an all-time high. But the truth is far less glamorous. I seem to struggle with everything that I had previously thought I had overcome, even though for the last eighteen years I have gotten up early and spent about an hour a day in devotional time with God.

I read my Bible through several times a year, move from translation to translation every couple of years to keep me sharp, have completed a doctoral degree in ministry, have tried fasting for long periods of time, and have written in a prayer journal daily. But even though I am doing what I think are all the right things, my spiritual sensitivity scale seems to register remarkably low.

The result is a life of incredible frustration. I keep trying to figure out God's will for my life, and as I press in to listen for that still, small Voice, all I seem to hear is static. My desire to do what God would have me do has often resulted in pulling out a pair of dice and rolling them. Worse, I find myself walking into a Chinese restaurant and waiting expectantly for the fortune cookie—as if God were going to send me a message creatively carved out just for me in the midst of sugar and flour. I cannot tell you how many times I have been disappointed with the fortune revealed in those cookies.

So, what gives? What am I doing wrong? Why do I have to remind my eyes to look away when a scantily dressed woman swaggers by? Why do I find myself reaching for prescription medicine during an overwhelming day? Why do I still lose my temper? Why do I often have trouble sleeping? What is the reason I worry about my daughter getting into college? After being married for twenty-four wonderful years, why do I sometimes get upset with my wife's actions? When I pray, why does it seem that some kryptonite keeps my prayers from being effective? And why do I find myself muttering words that as a kid I was taught never to say as I make my meager attempt to live for God with all that I have?

As a result of my spiritual journey, I thought it might be novel to simply share the truth (as I understand it). In a nutshell, it would go something like this: Life is often hard, and sometimes bad things happen that don't make sense. God is always in the mix—I am not sure how—and eventually this life will pass away and we will have a great shack in heaven.

Actually, that was fairly negative. Perhaps, if I tried again, I would say that I firmly believe that God is with me and because of that, even though things don't always make sense, I will never give up and will learn to treasure each moment as a gift. Doesn't that sound better?

It is my goal in this book to simply share a few thoughts about living the spiritual life. I am doing so not because I am perfect, but rather because I am embarrassed and ashamed of my past. I often wish that I could simply erase my brain in hopes that the yuck from my past would dissolve, as well. Yet it remains. I am who I am, and at this point, I can either wear my scars for God's glory or hide them in shame and guilt.

I was talking to a young woman with some scars of her own a couple of weeks ago, and I asked her, "What is the purpose of your scars?" The moment I asked her that question, I knew that I had to finish this little book about my life that I had been reluctantly chipping away at for the last nine years or so. To be honest with you, I am terrified of this little book because I don't want to be known as that guy with that past, but yet I also have to come to understand that because I have such a past, I can relate to people in a different manner. It is a gift—but one that was given through much pain and sorrow.

In taking an honest look at my journey, I want you to have hope that no matter where you find yourself, God can redeem and use you. Our Lord and Savior specializes in taking those who are messed up, burned out, and bypassed, and reclaiming them for His glory. Take a look at the prodigal son.

Michael Yaconelli writes,

> Look at the Bible. Its pages overflow with messy people. The biblical writers did not edit out the flaws of its heroes. Like Noah, for example. Everyone thought he was crazy. He certainly *was* a little strange, but Noah was also courageous, a man of great faith and strong will. Against the backdrop of unrelenting ridicule, Noah built a huge ark in the middle of the desert because God told him it was going to rain. No one believed him, but the rains did come and the flood happened, and after the water receded, Noah triumphantly left the boat, *got drunk and got naked.*
>
> What? *Drunk and naked?* I don't recall any of my Bible teachers or pastors talking about Noah's . . . uh . . . moment of indiscretion . . . er . . . weakness . . . um . . . failure. The Noah I've always heard about was fiercely faithful, irrepressibly independent, and relentlessly resolute. Noah was the model of great faith. Very few ever refer to Noah's losing battle with wine. Maybe being strong and faithful has its downside. Maybe for flood survivors life is more complicated than we would like to think, and maybe even Noah could have bouts of depression and loneliness.
>
> Why should I be surprised? Turns out *all* of the biblical characters were a complex mix of strengths and weaknesses. David, Abraham, Lot, Saul, Solomon, Rahab, and Sarah were God loving, courageous, brilliant, fearless, loyal, passionate, committed holy men and women who were also murderers, adulterers, and manic depressives.

They were men and women who could be gentle, holy, defenders of the faith one minute, and insecure, mentally unstable, unbelieving, shrewd, lying, grudge-holding tyrants the next. . . .

You might say Christianity has a tradition of messy spirituality. Messy prophets, messy kings, messy disciples, messy apostles.[1]

When I read these words, I was immediately intrigued with Yaconelli's journey. He saw the Bible as a compilation of messy people trying to live out lives of faith, but the reality was that most of them did not do so well. It gave me hope that I could be at least as good as some of those Bible folk. They reached up to the messy level. Perhaps—just perhaps—I could, as well.

The next time you feel as though God can't use you, just remember . . .

> Noah was a drunk.
> Abraham was too old.
> Isaac was a daydreamer.
> Jacob was a liar.
> Leah was ugly.
> Joseph was abused.
> Moses had a stuttering problem.
> Gideon was afraid.
> Samson had long hair and was a womanizer.
> Rahab was a prostitute.
> Jeremiah and Timothy were too young.
> David had an affair and was a murderer.
> Elijah was suicidal.
> Isaiah preached naked.
> Jonah ran from God.
> Naomi was a widow.
> Job went bankrupt.
> Peter denied Christ.
> The disciples fell asleep while praying.
> Martha worried about everything.

> Mary Magdalene was . . . well, you know . . .
> The Samaritan woman was divorced—more than once.
> Zacchaeus was too small.
> Saul was too religious.
> Timothy had an ulcer . . . *and*
> Lazarus was dead!

The Bible is full of characters—like you and me—upon whom God shined the spotlight so that we could see how they overcame overwhelming situations. The Bible gives hope to us all because it reveals a pathway of usefulness and grace. We are imperfect people who are simply trying to live for Jesus in a complicated world—and it is indeed complicated. The questions of ethics, sexuality, church . . . who knows the right answers?

Yet, through it all, God is good, God is love, God has the power, and we have hope.

---

1. Michael Yaconelli, *Messy Spirituality* (Grand Rapids, MI: Zondervan, 2002), 13–15; emphasis in original.

If you enjoyed *Never Give Up*, you'll also want to read these great stories of God's providence.

The Prodigal Daughter
by Kay D. Rizzo

The Prodigal Daughter is based on the true story of a young and gifted woman who leaves home amid the protests and tears of her father. Headstrong and determined to become a star, Brianna soon finds herself swept into a world far different from the life of fame and riches she'd expected. As her dreams begin to crumble, little does she realize the horror into which she is about to plunge. Like Jesus' story of another errant child, *The Prodigal Daughter* portrays a father's love and reminds us of how far our heavenly Father will go in order to redeem and restore His lost children.
Perfect Bound, 160 Pages
ISBN 13: 978-0-8163-5420-7

Backstage Pass
by Naomi Striemer

Eighteen-year-old Naomi stepped into one of the most prestigious board rooms known to musicians—Sony Records—and walked out a few minutes later with a record deal. Naomi was hailed by critics as "the next Celine Dion." But one conversation changed it all. *Backstage Pass* is the candid account of an up-and-coming recording artist who left everything to follow Christ.
Perfect Bound, 192 Pages
ISBN 13: 978-0-8163-4518-2

Kidnapped!
by Greg Budd

This is no ordinary story, and Paul Ratsara is no ordinary man. Raised in poverty and darkness, Paul Ratsara is a living example of the remarkable deliverance and transformation that a relationship with Christ brings. Every chapter radiates with confidence in a miracle-working God, who is bigger than our problems and greater than our difficulties.
Perfect Bound, 160 Pages
ISBN 13: 978-0-8163-4676-9

Pacific Press®
Publishing Association
"Where the Word Is Life"

Three ways to order:

1	Local	Adventist Book Center®
2	Call	1-800-765-6955
3	Shop	AdventistBookCenter.com

AdventistBookCenter.com | AdventistBookCenter | @AdventistBooks | YouTube AdventistBooks